CHINA IN AFRICA: THE NEW COLONIALISM?

HEARING

BEFORE THE

SUBCOMMITTEE ON AFRICA, GLOBAL HEALTH, GLOBAL HUMAN RIGHTS, AND INTERNATIONAL ORGANIZATIONS

OF THE

COMMITTEE ON FOREIGN AFFAIRS
HOUSE OF REPRESENTATIVES

ONE HUNDRED FIFTEENTH CONGRESS

SECOND SESSION

MARCH 7, 2018

Serial No. 115–117

Printed for the use of the Committee on Foreign Affairs

Available via the World Wide Web: http://www.foreignaffairs.house.gov/ or
http://www.gpo.gov/fdsys/

U.S. GOVERNMENT PUBLISHING OFFICE

28–876PDF   WASHINGTON : 2018

CONTENTS

CHINA IN AFRICA: THE NEW COLONIALISM?

WEDNESDAY, MARCH 7, 2018

House of Representatives,
Subcommittee on Africa, Global Health,
Global Human Rights, and International Organizations,
Committee on Foreign Affairs,
Washington, DC.

The subcommittee met, pursuant to notice, at 2:00 p.m., in room 2172 Rayburn House Office Building, Hon. Christopher H. Smith (chairman of the subcommittee) presiding.

Mr. SMITH. The subcommittee will come to order, and good afternoon to everybody. Thank you for being here.

Today's hearing will analyze China's activity and engagement in sub-Saharan Africa. In particular, we will look into what motivates China and how Chinese involvement has affected African countries.

While a number of African nations have welcomed Chinese engagement and investment, it often comes at a very high cost, with a focus on extractive industries, entanglement with neomercantilist trade policy, and a tendency to adopt the worst practices that prop up kleptocrats and autocrats such as DR Congo's Joseph Kabila, while fueling corruption in an effort to win contracts.

China's engagement in Africa was once driven by revolutionary ideology motivated by competition with the Soviet Union as much as it was directed at "capitalist roaders" aligned with the United States.

In Angola, for example, in 1975, Soviet-backed communists bested Chinese-backed revolutionary rivals including Jonas Savimbi, who was a Maoist before he was reborn in the 1980s as an anti-communist freedom fighter.

Today, China's one-time Marxist-Leninist-Maoist impulse has been softened to the point of almost—but not quite—disappearing, with revolution replaced by infrastructure projects, trade missions, soft loans, and scholarships for promising African students, all part of the ubiquitous Beijing effort at hegemony.

While on the one hand, Africa needs investment and it needs infrastructure, we see a worrisome trend of African countries sliding into indebtedness to China, accumulating burdens that may be beyond their capacity to meet.

All too often, the roads China builds are meant to allow it access to mineral resources that it can extract and ship to China, or are a part of the One-Belt, One-Road initiative, which is designed to benefit China and, ultimately, help it project power.

(1)

Further, as anyone who has been to Africa has observed, these grand construction projects often utilize Chinese engineers and workers and not Africans. I remember being in the capital of DR Congo on one of many trips to Africa and seeing a large number of Chinese workers. They looked very happy. I thought they probably were Laogai prisoners who were there working, and they didn't even look up during the hour of observation by myself and a member of our Embassy staff.

As we will hear today, nowhere in Africa is the problem of indebtedness more pronounced than in Djibouti, a strategically important country in the Horn of Africa which sits astride the Mandeb Strait and one of only five African countries where Secretary of State Tillerson is visiting on his trip to Africa this week.

A former French colony, Djibouti hosts a French military base and an American one, and Djibouti also hosts, as of last summer, China's only permanent military base outside of China.

China's overall foreign aid and financial leverage on the continent has been difficult to quantify—as has demonstrating how that translates into influence.

Yeoman work in this regard has been done by Aid Data at the College of William and Mary, which had written testimony to be submitted as part of the record, without objection. It demonstrates a correlation between how an African country votes at the United Nations General Assembly and how much aid it receives from China. There is a quid pro quo.

Another strategically important country with high indebtedness to China that the Secretary will visit is Ethiopia. It is also a country where China has most clearly aligned itself with repressive forces.

In addition to assisting the government in controlling information flows, such as jamming the Voice of America and BBC broadcasts, the Chinese Communist Party has engaged with Ethiopia's ruling party in "training and exchanges." And just recently, we held yet another hearing on the brutality by the Ethiopians in this subcommittee.

At the Brookings Institution, as it has documented, cadres from the ruling Ethiopian People's Revolutionary Democratic Front were "taught" comprehensively how to manage their own organizational structure, ideological work propaganda system, and cadre education.

Thus, it seems, ideology still matters with regard to how China engages with Africa. It is no coincidence that Ethiopia has become one of the most repressive regimes on the continent and the subject of a House resolution focused on Ethiopia's abusive practices that Ms. Bass and I have sponsored, H. Res. 128.

Whereas the U.S. emphasizes good governance, it suits China's interest to train its partners in old-style Leninism. We have also received testimony from one of our witnesses on how China projects power in the form of Confucius Institutes located in close to 40 African nations, and I would point out parenthetically that as co-chairman of the China Commission, I've had hearings and requested a GAO report on Confucius Institutes in this country.

There are well over 100. They have a disproportionate impact. Their teachers carry with them the ideology of Beijing, and to the receiving universities and colleges they are often seen as just another addition—free money, if you will—but with a very, very significant cost because it is a projection of soft power.

This subcommittee has held hearings on how China has used these to push the Sino-centric narrative, again, which aligns with Communist Party propaganda, and totally curtails academic freedom.

In addition to utilizing Confucius Institutes, they train Mandarin speakers and indoctrinate students with a pro-China world view. China is expanding its media presence in Africa.

Kenya is the country with the largest penetration of Chinese media and the highest level of brand recognition, according to our Broadcasting Board of Governors, which overseas the Voice of America, and which recently conducted a survey of China's media presence in Africa.

It should be noted that, of the five major international networks in Kenya, China's news broadcasts were the least—I say again, least, trusted.

There is also a thought for Voice of America and the Broadcasting Board of Governors to consider—add Mandarin programming to the repertoire of languages in which you broadcast in Africa. By broadcasting objective news stories in Mandarin, you will expose not only African students learning Mandarin to more truthful media, but you will be able to reach the estimated 1 million or so Chinese living or working in Africa with news that they are otherwise unable to access.

China is also Kenya's largest bilateral lender. Kenya is one of the three highest debtor nations to China in Africa, along with Djibouti and Ethiopia. It is also a country where Secretary Tillerson will be visiting.

On his trip he may want to highlight the following anecdote, which I believe aptly contrasts China's African engagement with that of the United States.

Health commodities supplied by the U.S. Agency for International Development, including lifesaving antiretrovirals distributed as part of our PEPFAR program and antimalarial commodities, used to be shipped to and stored in a warehouse near Nairobi for distribution, not only throughout Kenya, but also neighboring East African countries as well.

Then in July 2013, Kenya's Parliament proposed a 1½ percent levy on all imports to Kenya to help pay for the nearly $4 billion railroad from the Port of Mombasa to Nairobi built by the state-owned China Road and Bridge Corporation.

Donated goods including antiretrovirals for Kenyans living and coping with HIV/AIDS were subject to this levy to help pay Kenya's debt to China.

As a result of this, the flow of lifesaving commodities into Kenya and neighboring countries was burdened and slowed. Kenya's ministry of health offered to step in and pay the levy. But their payments were often delayed by some 2 months. Meanwhile, charges attributed to clearance delays continued to accrue and had to be paid by the United States taxpayer.

Ultimately, over a year later, Kenya's Parliament amended the legislation to exclude donated goods from the Chinese railway payment levy. But the damage had been done.

Today, due to this experience and other factors related to logistics and a new USAID implementation partner, USAID no longer uses a warehouse in Kenya. Storage and distribution has been moved offshore to a location that's centrally located and, one hopes, less prone to disruption.

I close with a number of questions. How did this warehouse episode, borne out of Kenya's need to repay debt to China, benefit Kenyans suffering from HIV/AIDS?

How did it affect the ability of Kenya to serve as a regional distribution hub for East Africa with all the collateral economic benefits that accrue from the purely humanitarian initiative paid for by the United States taxpayer?

More broadly, where is China's PEPFAR or the equivalent of the President's malaria initiative? These are questions and more that we on the subcommittee will have for this very, very distinguished group of panelists.

But before going to them, I'd like to yield to my good friend and colleague, the ranking member, Ms. Bass.

Ms. BASS. Thank you, Mr. Chairman.

Once again, you are calling an important hearing to examine China's economic and political impact in Africa. The title of this hearing raises the question as to whether or not China should be viewed as the new colonial power within the continent of Africa.

I am very much concerned about that as well, especially with regard to labor, given the need for employment on the continent and the recurring disputes about wages and the treatment of workers.

There are also concerns about the extractive nature of China's engagement and what is now being referred to as debt-trap diplomacy. This concept poses the question of whether developing countries are mortgaging their resources and strategic assets to China. If there is a drop in commodity prices and countries have difficulties with these loans, they might get caught in a debt trap that leaves them vulnerable to China's influence. These are critical issues and that I will expect to be addressed throughout the hearing.

A recent Atlantic Council report entitled, "Escaping China's Shadow: Finding America's Competitive Edge in Africa," argued that the presence of Chinese companies does not preclude American business success.

So I hope that our discussion today will shed light on the fact that U.S. companies can and should be doing business in Africa. Some people suggest that China shouldn't be in Africa.

But instead of going down that road, I would rather say that the U.S. should step up our involvement. If we are concerned about the Chinese, then where are we?

There is a major infrastructure deficit across the African continent. African countries need roads, hospitals, school buildings, and other vital infrastructure and China is currently filling that need.

But the United States can, too. But we should do so in a responsible fashion that benefits African countries and U.S. businesses, and African nations want to partner with U.S. businesses.

In fact, the President of Ghana was just in the United States and one of his goals in coming here was to encourage investment and partnership in order to develop a relationship with the United States that is characterized by increased trade and investment cooperation.

We should remember that as we seek to promote U.S. trade and direct investment in Africa, we are also creating opportunities for African growth so that the African middle class can help create societies that are no longer dependent on foreign aid.

The chairman and I, as well as the full committee chairman, Chairman Royce, have worked on a number of initiatives that really begin to reframe how we do foreign aid such as Feed the Future, Mr. Chairman, and Electrify Africa, where we are promoting our business involvement with the goal of African nations not being dependent on foreign aid.

I also hope that our discussion today will highlight areas of common interest between the United States and China in Africa that could provide the basis for enhanced bilateral and multilateral cooperation, particularly on important conflict mediation priorities across the continent.

So my goal for this hearing, therefore, is to be forward thinking in how we view China's engagement across Africa. We must continue to stay focused on U.S. policy toward Africa by partnering with African nations and deepening our engagement with African civil society, especially the next generation of leaders because rest assured, if the United States loses focus, other countries are more than happy to fill any gap left behind by the U.S.

So I look forward to this hearing, look forward to our distinguished witnesses on how the U.S. can help achieve these objectives.

Mr. Chair, I yield back.

Mr. SMITH. Thank you very much.

We now go to Ambassador Rooney. Any opening comments?

Mr. ROONEY. I am not on the committee but I'd like to thank Chairman Smith for letting me come and learn a little bit more about Africa.

I've been in 100 countries and Africa is the one part of the world I freely admit I know the least of. So I've been reading your material and look forward to your testimony.

Thank you very much.

Mr. SMITH. Thank you, Mr. Ambassador.

I'd like to now yield to Dr. Bera.

Mr. BERA. Thank you, Mr. Chairman, and to the ranking member, not just for the hearing, but also for your leadership in making sure Congress stays interested in the continent of Africa.

You know, I absolutely look forward to the witness testimony as well as getting more information and, you know, when we were with Ambassador Green yesterday and just thinking about where USAID is going and, you know, given his history in Africa as well, I know our aid and development work really is looking at capacity building and helping look at the unique resources in the countries that we are going into and trying to move toward capacity building. And I'd be really interested in hearing from the witnesses because when I think about China's involvement and, you know, we welcome that foreign direct investment into the—into Africa and other developing countries.

You know, our worry though is China is—you know, with that foreign direct investment, it's Chinese companies that are building a lot of that infrastructure, Chinese workers that are benefitting from that as opposed to looking at the workforce in the countries that they are developing, helping them develop their own capacity.

And the chairman and the ranking member have already touched on the impact of the loans and the loan repayment and what that has in terms of the African countries' and the recipient countries' ability to, again, care for themselves.

So, again, thank you for this hearing. I'm looking forward to the testimony and, you know, again, perhaps if you all can touch on the contrast between U.S. and Western approach to aid and development versus the Chinese approach.

So thank you, and I yield back.

Mr. SMITH. Thank you very much, Dr. Bera.

I'd like to now introduce our very distinguished panel, beginning first with Gordon Chang, who I have listened to for years on radio and, as a matter of fact, I asked that he be here because I am so impressed with his incisiveness, but also much of what he has written.

He is the author of the "Coming Collapse of China" and "Nuclear Showdown: North Korea Takes on the World" and a columnist for The Daily Beast. He's also an expert on China and northeast Asia. Mr. Chang lived and worked in China and Hong Kong for almost two decades, most recently in Shanghai.

He has spoken at a number of colleges and universities and given briefings to government entities such as the National Intelligence Council, Central Intelligence Agency, State Department, and the Pentagon.

His writings have appeared in news outlets such as The New York Times, the Wall Street Journal, and the Weekly Standard, and Mr. Chang has testified before the Foreign Affairs Committee and the U.S.-China Economic and Security Review Commission. So we welcome him back to Capitol Hill and look forward to his expert analysis on this important topic.

We will then hear from Mr. Joshua Meservey, who is a senior policy analyst for Africa and the Middle East at the Heritage Foundation. A former Peace Corps volunteer in Zambia, he specializes in counterinsurgency, non-state-armed groups in security development's nexus.

Prior to joining the Heritage Foundation, Mr. Meservey worked in the Church World Services Refugee Resettlement Operation in Kenya as well as the U.S. Army Special Operations Command in the Atlantic Council's Africa Center. He has testified before the Senate and is a frequent commentator on African policy issues in a range of print and digital media outlets. We welcome him as well.

We will then hear from Scott Morris, who's a senior fellow at the Center for Global Development and director of the U.S. Development Policy Initiative. Prior to joining the Center for Global Development, Mr. Morris served as Deputy Assistant Secretary for Development, Finance, and Debt at the U.S. Treasury Department during the first term of the Obama administration.

In that capacity, he has led U.S. engagement with a number of international financial institutions, such as the World Bank, American Development Bank, and the African Development Bank.

He has also represented the U.S. Government in the G-20's Development Working Group and was the Treasury's plus-one on the board of the Millennium Challenge Corporation.

Before his post at the U.S. Treasury, Mr. Morris was a senior staff member of the Financial Services Committee of the U.S. House where he was responsible for the committee's international policy issues.

It should be noted that Mr. Morris was asked last minute to fill in for the witness, although on his own right we are very, very happy to have him. So I thank him for coming at such short notice.

And then we will hear from Anita Plummer, who's an assistant professor of African studies whose research focuses on African political economy, emerging markets, transnationalism, and Sino-African relations.

Her current book project, "Close Encounters: Street-Level Perspective on Kenya and China," examines local, national, and transnational narratives in South-South cooperation.

Before joining the faculty at Howard, Dr. Plummer taught international studies at Spelman College. She was a Mellon post-doctoral fellow in the Cultures and Transnational Perspective program and visiting assistant professor of global studies and political science at the University of California, Los Angeles.

She's also a fellow at the Carter G. Woodson Center, a pre-doctoral fellow at the University of Virginia. Dr. Plummer received her Ph.D. from Howard in Washington.

So if I could now, Gordon Chang, you have the floor.

STATEMENT OF MR. GORDON CHANG, AUTHOR

Mr. CHANG. Chairman Smith, Ranking Member Bass, and distinguished members of the committee, thank you very much for this opportunity.

My testimony focuses on China's views on sub-Saharan Africa, especially in relationship to Beijing's expanding ambitions and I also look at this in the context of colonialism.

I conclude that China is practicing a new form of colonialism and that China's relations with Africa threaten Americans' interests.

Beijing looks at Africa as special. For instance, it says that more than half of its foreign assistance goes to the continent.

Now, Beijing, obviously, wants favors in return and, clearly, there is this strong connection between what a country will do for China and the amount of aid that it receives.

China needs African support for a number of things but especially because Xi Jinping, the foreign leader, wants to show that he is the commanding voice of the developing world.

At one time, Beijing denied that it provided any sort of model for the developing world, but now it brags about it and has even branded it, calling it socialism with Chinese characteristics for a new era.

Xi Jinping, however, has ambitions beyond just assisting the developing world. There are indications that he believes that not only should China's model be the world's model but that China's leader be the world's leader.

China, in its pronouncements recently, is making the case that it should be the world's only sovereign, a view that Chinese emperors maintained, and that, of course, brings us to China's relationships with Africa.

Now, Beijing vehemently denies, as some influential African voices say, that China is practicing a form of colonialism, or neocolonialism.

Nonetheless, Beijing's use of this imperial-era language is inconsistent with the denial of its colonial ambitions. China, if it were free to implement its imperial system, would divest all other nations of sovereignty and that, of course, is the essence of colonialism.

The Chinese leadership, unfortunately, holds views that foster colonial mentality in the Chinese capital and there are two of these that I'd like to just briefly mention.

First of all, Chinese leaders have this view of a brutish conception of the world where the strong do what they want and the weak must comply.

Second of all, to make matters worse, Chinese officials give the impression that they view African people as inferior to their own. This was made painfully obvious during a 14-minute skit last month on China's Central Television at the Spring Gala.

The skit, which was seen by some 800 million viewers, depicted Kenyans as objects of derision and even as subhuman. It is therefore hard to think that China's leaders see Africans as equals and these perceptions of inequality fuel the notion that they must hold neocolonial attitudes.

African nations, at least at first glance, are dealing with China freely, and so therefore, China, of course, is not practicing a 19th century type of colonialism.

Yet, of course, in our world, the nature of colonialism is changing, and China, by basing troops on the continent, by corrupting officials, by flooding local markets with Chinese manufactured goods, by sending workers to Africa, by straining local economies with trade imbalances, as well as by swamping countries in debt, which Ranking Member Bass mentioned in her opening remarks, have now begun to dominate the continent.

Once it locks in countries and makes them dependent, Beijing gets their support for geopolitical goals and one of these goals is undermining democracy.

Africa is struggling to shake off the rule of the so-called "big men" and it doesn't need any more failing states like China-supported Zimbabwe.

Now as the Zimbabwe example shows, Beijing is affecting the course of African development at a crucial period of its history. Some people believe that the United States doesn't have interests in Africa.

Even if this were true, and it's not, but even if it were true, Africa gives China the ability to threaten the American homeland.

As Chairman Smith mentioned, the Chinese now have a military base in Djibouti, their first overseas one, but they also want one at Walvis Bay in the South Atlantic.

The Chinese leaders have even been thinking about taking over an air base in the Azores. From the Azores, China would be able to control the mouth of the Mediterranean and their planes would be closer to New York than Pearl Harbor is to Los Angeles.

A belligerent China in Asia is bad enough. A dangerous one close to our shores would be far worse.

Thank you.

[The prepared statement of Mr. Chang follows:]

**Statement of
Gordon G. Chang**

**Subcommittee on
Africa, Global Health, Global Human Rights, and International
Organizations
House Committee on Foreign Affairs**

China in Africa: The New Colonialism?

March 7, 2018

Chairman Smith, Ranking Member Bass, and distinguished Members of the Committee:

It is a privilege for me to appear before you today, and I thank you for this opportunity.

My name is Gordon Guthrie Chang. I am a writer and live in Bedminster, New Jersey.

I worked as a lawyer in Hong Kong from 1981-1991 and in Shanghai from 1996-2001. Between these two periods, I frequently traveled to Asia from California. I regularly go to Asia now.

I am the author of *The Coming Collapse of China* (Random House, 2001) and *Nuclear Showdown: North Korea Takes On the World* (Random House, 2006).

I now write regularly about China, North Korea, and the rest of Asia for The Daily Beast, The National Interest, and other publications.

This testimony looks at how China views Sub-Saharan Africa, especially with regard to Beijing's expanding strategic ambitions. I discuss these points in the context of colonialism.

I conclude that Xi Jinping, the Chinese ruler, believes his country should be the world's only sovereign state, which is the essence of colonialism, and that today his country's relations with Africa resemble a new form of colonialism.

Moreover, I believe Xi's ambitions for Africa, however one characterizes them, threaten America.

Africa's Special Position in the Chinese World

In official statements, Beijing maintains all nations are equals, and it says China seeks friendly relations with all.

Chinese leaders, however, consider Africa special. That special status is one the continent enjoyed from the first years of the People's Republic when Mao Zedong, the founder of the regime, looked far afield for support in his various struggles with Moscow for leadership of the communist bloc.

These days, Beijing still keeps ties with the continent warm. It has been, for instance, a tradition of China's leaders to go to Africa on their first trips abroad. Xi Jinping visited Tanzania, South Africa, and the Republic of the Congo during his initial trip as the country's president, in March 2013. There is no year when high-ranking Chinese officials do not make high-profile visits to the continent.

And Beijing does not neglect handouts in maintaining the relationship. Beijing claims that more than half of its foreign aid goes to Africa.

Beijing obviously wants favors in return from African states, and not just them providing a reliable supply of raw materials and ready markets for China's manufactures. Increasingly, Beijing seeks support for its geopolitical goals. Foreign Minister Wang Yi hinted at that last month in Beijing. "Both sides have always thought that China and the African Union should speak with a common voice and coordinate a common position on the world stage," he said at the seventh round of the China-African Union Strategic Dialogue.[1] Elizabeth Manero, writing in the Harvard Political Review, noted that "there is a strong correlation between the amount of aid given, and the support for China's foreign policy objectives."[2]

China needs African support because Xi Jinping wants to show he is the commanding voice of the developing world. At one time, Beijing denied it provided a model for others, but now China's leader openly boasts about it.

The world heard China promote its model during Xi's 203-minute Work Report, delivered at the 19th National Communist Party Congress last October. "It offers a new option for other countries and nations who want to speed up their development while preserving their independence," Xi said, referring to his model, branded as "Socialism with Chinese Characteristics for a New Era."[3]

Xi, however, has ambitions beyond helping the developing world. There are indications he in fact believes that not only should China's model be the world's model but also that China's leader should be the world's leader.

Xi suggests the world would be peaceful if Beijing ruled "All Under Heaven." This *tianxia* worldview, which underpinned two millennia of Chinese history under the emperors, is increasingly evident in China's pronouncements and imagery and is of course fundamentally inconsistent with the existence of a multitude of sovereign states. So when Xi speaks about "a community of common destiny," he is most likely thinking of China's rich imperial past and suggesting he should hold sway over all domains, near and far.

The notion of China controlling the entire world is breathtaking—not to mention ludicrous—but Beijing's house scholars actively study the application of the *tianxia* system to the entire planet and Chinese officials offer it up in public for consideration, as Fei-Ling Wang of the Georgia Institute of Technology notes in a new book, *The China Order: Centralia, World Empire, and the Nature of Chinese Power.*

Xi, for instance, increasingly employs *tianxia* language in his pronouncements. "The Chinese have always held that the world is united and all under heaven are one family," he declared in his 2017 New Year's Message.[4]

Moreover, Foreign Minister Wang, in *Study Times*, the Central Party School newspaper, last September wrote that Xi Jinping's "thought on diplomacy" "has made innovations on and transcended the traditional Western theories of international relations for the past 300 years."[5] Wang with his time reference is almost certainly pointing to the system of sovereign states, which traces its roots to the Treaty of Westphalia of 1648.

Wang's use of "transcended," consequently, hints that Xi wants a world without sovereign states—or at least no more than one of them. China, in these and other pronouncements, is now making the case that it should be the world's only sovereign, the view that Chinese emperors maintained.

The trend of recent comments warns us that China does not want to live within the current Westphalian system or even to adjust it. Its leaders, from every indication, are thinking of replacing it altogether. Chinese words, therefore, appear ominous, not benign, a signal that China will try to do away with what is seen as Westphalia's cacophony with *tianxia*'s orderliness.

And that brings us to China's relationships with African nations. Beijing vehemently denies, as some influential Africans charge, that it is practicing colonialism or neo-colonialism on the continent. "We absolutely will not take the old path of Western colonists, and we absolutely will not sacrifice Africa's ecological environment and long-term interests," Wang Yi in 2015 said to Chinese state broadcaster China Central Television while visiting Kenya.[6]

Nonetheless, Beijing's frequent use of *tianxia* language is inconsistent with its denials of colonial ambitions. China, if it could implement the *tianxia* system it is promoting, would divest all other states, including African ones, of sovereignty. That, of course, would be the essence of colonialism.

Beijing's Views Today

Xi Jinping's imperial pretentions tell us he wants to be a colonial master, but is he one today?

The Chinese leadership, unfortunately, holds views that foster colonial relations. There are two in particular. First, China's current crop of leaders have a brutish conception of the world.

"China is a big country and other countries are small countries, and that's just a fact," said Yang Jiechi in July 2010.[7] If there is one sentence that sums up how Beijing in fact views the international system, Yang's arrogant assertion, part of an extraordinary half-hour rant, is it.

Yang, then China's foreign minister, did not have Africa in mind while uttering those contemptuous words—he was in Hanoi and glaring at his counterpart from Singapore at the time—but China still looks at Africa in the same way it perceives Singapore—less powerful than mighty China.

Second, to make matters worse, Chinese officials surely see African people as inferior to their own kind. That was painfully evident last month in the 14-minute skit on China Central Television's Spring Festival Gala, the premier television show in China. In "Let's Celebrate Together," a Chinese actress in blackface played the part of a Kenyan mother, who had an enormous bosom and ridiculously large buttocks. Worse, her sidekick was a human-size monkey.[8] The skit was intended to praise Xi Jinping's signature One Belt One Road initiative.

Kenyans, not to mention some Chinese viewers, were outraged at the racist and derogatory depictions of Africans. In recent years, there have been many ugly portrayals of Africans in Chinese media, and although this was not the worst—by no means was it so—this sketch was striking because China Central Television, by airing this to about 800 million viewers, made it clear Chinese officials think of Africans as objects of derision and even subhuman. And because the skit was carried by the state broadcaster, this view of Africans is apparently shared by the Beijing leadership, which, alarmingly, is making more frequent race-based appeals to the Chinese people.

It is, therefore, hard to think that China's leaders see Africans as equals, and perceptions of inequality suggests they also hold neo-colonial attitudes. The skit, after all, showed patronizing Chinese helping poor Africans who "loved" China because of all the good things it provided Africa.

As a result of the skit, Africans are talking even more about Chinese racism and colonialism. The *Daily Nation*, the leading Nairobi newspaper, quoted a Kenyan student asking "whether Kenya is truly a valuable trade partner to China or just another cow they are milking."[9]

That is the critical question. African nations, at least at first glance, are trading and accepting Beijing's investment and aid freely. The relationship is not colonial in the 19th century sense of the concept, and African states have retained their sovereignty.

Yet the nature of colonialism has been changing. So what is the concept today?

Beijing, perhaps inadvertently, last month revealed a two-part test for colonialism as it rebutted comments from Secretary of State Rex Tillerson that China was a "new imperial power" in Latin America. The *Global Times*, the tabloid controlled by *People's Daily*, said in an editorial that Latin American countries were trading and doing business with China of their own "free will" and "for mutual benefit" and that "China has no military bases in the region and has dispatched no troops to any of the Latin American countries."[10]

China may not be an imperial power in Latin America, but in Africa it could be according to the *Global Times* formulation. First, some of the dealings between Beijing and African states seems to be tainted by both corruption and subtle forms of coercion, thereby undercutting African free will.

Second, China established its first overseas military base last year, in Djibouti. Many expect a second one, in Walvis Bay in Namibia, in the not too distant future. Beijing has sent "peacekeepers"—troops—to South Sudan under the U.N. banner.

There are, of course, other definitions of colonialism. "Imperialism, for me, inevitably involves some form of foreign domination, which results in substantially altering the target population or polity; either gradually or suddenly it loses the ability to resist," wrote acclaimed journalist Howard French in *China's Second Continent: How a Million Migrants Are Building a New Empire in Africa*. "In *The Abacus and the Sword*, his account of Japan's takeover of Korea, which was launched at the end of the nineteenth century, Peter Duus wrote that imperialism requires 'an available victim—a weaker, less organized, or less advanced society or state unable to defend itself against outside intrusion.' "[11]

The French-Duus formulation, which is as broad as the definition can get and still retain meaning, makes China look like a colonial power in Africa. As an initial matter, there are the Chinese-created moral hazards. Although Beijing provides "no-strings-attached" and low-interest loans—what looks like the apparent opposite of colonization—this easy money encourages governments to spend irresponsibly, creating the debt crises of the future. "China is co-opting states into its sphere of influence by burying them in debt," writes New Delhi-based China watcher Brahma Chellaney. The title of his article from last month says it all: "China Ensnares Vulnerable States in a Debt Trap."[12] At the moment, China is trying to renegotiate loans made imprudently to Zambia.

With the enticement of low-cost loans, Beijing gets the opportunity to corrupt officials, obtain the rights to extract minerals and hydrocarbons, flood local markets with manufactured goods, send its workers to Africa, and strain local economies with trade imbalances.

Beijing has, in part by happenstance, developed what French calls "a kind of modern-day barter system" by which Chinese enterprises build infrastructure with payment in the form of natural resources.[13]

Once it locks in countries and makes them dependent, Beijing gains support for its geopolitical goals. One of those goals is the undermining of democracy and the consequent fortification of authoritarianism.

China, in short, is spreading its economic and political model to Africa. In some places this Chinese system has benefitted local populations, and in others it has not. Africa, struggling to shake off the misrule of the so-called "big men," does not need any more failing states like China-supported Zimbabwe.

As the Zimbabwe example shows, Beijing is affecting the course of African development at a crucial moment in its history. "This is going to determine Africa's future for the next fifty years," Ed Brown, an executive at one of Ghana's think tanks, told French, referring to the relationship with China. "The big question is whether African countries are dynamic enough to take advantage, or whether they'll end up being the appendage of somebody else all over again."[14]

Africa's economy is mostly vibrant as is its demography. Therefore, the region should do well as long as politics does not get in the way. The risk is that Africa becomes a Chinese appendage and falls back, failing to meet its great potential.

For some African countries, mid-century will be an inflection point when population peaks and natural resources run out. The next three decades, consequently, will be crucial. The challenge for these nations will be to take advantage of what Beijing offers without being held hostage to Chinese designs for them.

America's Stake

Some, like William Hawkins, believe America does not have many interests in Africa to defend.[15] Even if that is true, the U.S., with global reach and responsibilities, has a general stake in the success of all parts of the world, both from economic and security points of view.

We prosper, despite what many think, when other portions of the planet also do well. China, because its relations with Africa are often predatory, can stunt growth there.

And, whatever one may think, there is one crucial interest all Americans have in Africa. Africa gives China the ability to threaten the U.S. homeland. Beijing wants a military base at Walvis Bay, and China's leaders have long looked at raising their red flag over the Atlantic off the African coast. In the Azores, specifically the island of Terceira, Chinese aircraft could control the mouth of the Mediterranean and would be closer to New York than Pearl Harbor is to Los Angeles.[16]

Hawkins may or may not be right about a lack of immediate American interests, but there is no sense in ignoring the potential implications of Chinese control of Africa. A belligerent China in Asia is bad enough. A dangerous China much closer to our shores is far worse.

1   "Wang Yi: In the Historic Process of Africa Standing Up, Getting Stronger, China Willing to Be Africa's Most Reliable Strategic Partner," Ministry of Foreign Affairs, February 8, 2018, http://www.fmprc.gov.cn/web/wjbzhd/t1533145.shtml.

2   Elizabeth Manero, "China's Investment in Africa: The New Colonialism?" Harvard Political Review, February 3, 2017, http://harvardpolitics.com/world/chinas-investment-in-africa-the-new-colonialism/.

3   Xi Jinping, "Secure a Decisive Victory in Building a Moderately Prosperous Society in All Respects and Strive for the Great Success of Socialism with Chinese Characteristics for a New Era," 19th National Congress of the Communist Party of China, October 18, 2017, http://www.xinhuanet.com/english/download/Xi_Jinping's_report_at_19th_CPC_National_Congress.pdf.

4   "Chairman Xi Jinping's 2017 New Year's Message," Xinhua News Agency, December 31, 2016, http://news.xinhuanet.com/politics/2016-12/31/c_1120227034.htm.

5   Ministry of Foreign Affairs, "Forge Ahead Under the Guidance of General Secretary Xi Jinping's Thought on Diplomacy," September 1, 2017, http://www.fmprc.gov.cn/mfa_eng/zxxx_662805/t1489143.shtml. For more, see "China Says Xi Transcends West as a Diplomatic 'Pioneer,' " Reuters, September 1, 2017, https://www.reuters.com/article/us-china-congress-diplomacy/china-says-xi-transcends-west-as-a-diplomatic-pioneer-idUSKCN1BC4KQ.

6   "China Will Not Take Path of 'Western Colonists' in Africa—Foreign Minister," Reuters, January 12, 2015, https://www.reuters.com/article/china-africa/china-will-not-take-path-of-western-colonists-in-africa-foreign-minister-idUSL3N0UR1J920150112.

7   John Pomfret, "U.S. Takes a Tougher Tone with China," *Washington Post*, July 30, 2010, http://www.washingtonpost.com/wp-dyn/content/article/2010/07/29/AR2010072906416.html.

8   *See* James Wilkinson, " 'Racist' Chinese Spring Festival Gala TV Show Causes Uproar Over 'Blackface' and 'Big Bottoms,' " *South China Morning Post* (Hong Kong), February 16, 2018, http://www.scmp.com/news/china/society/article/2133558/racist-chinese-spring-festival-gala-tv-show-causes-consternation.

9   Elvis Ondieki, "Chinese Embassy Denies Racism in 'Blackface' Skit," *Daily Nation* (Nairobi), February 18, 2018, https://www.nation.co.ke/news/Chinese-embassy-denies-racism-in-skit-Lunar-New-Year/1056-4310180-y1uiew/index.html.

10   "Tillerson Shows Disdain for China's Constructive Approach to Latin America," editorial, *Global Times* (Beijing), February 3, 2018, http://www.globaltimes.cn/content/1087971.shtml.

11   Howard W. French, *China's Second Continent: How a Million Migrants Are Building a New Empire in Africa* (New York: Vintage Books, 2015), p. 259.

12   Brahma Chellaney, "China Ensnares Vulnerable States in a Debt Trap," *Nikkei Asian Review*, February 20, 2018, https://asia.nikkei.com/Viewpoints/Brahma-Chellaney/China-ensnares-vulnerable-states-in-a-debt-trap.

13   French, *China's Second Continent*, p. 4.

14   Ibid., p. 8.

15   *See* William R. Hawkins, "A Minor U.S. Role in Africa," Family Security Matters, November 17, 2017, http://www.familysecuritymatters.org/publications/detail/a-minor-us-role-in-africa.

16   *See* Gordon G. Chang, "Red Flag Over the Atlantic," *National Review*, November 4, 2012, https://www.nationalreview.com/2012/11/red-flag-over-atlantic-gordon-g-chang/.

Mr. SMITH. Thank you, Mr. Chang.

I would like to now go to Mr. Meservey.

STATEMENT OF MR. JOSHUA MESERVEY, SENIOR POLICY ANALYST, AFRICA AND THE MIDDLE EAST, THE HERITAGE FOUNDATION

Mr. MESERVEY. Chairman Smith, Ranking Member Bass, and members of the committee, thank you for this opportunity to testify.

Thank you as well for highlighting one of the most important issues facing Africa and, by extension, U.S. interests in Africa.

With your permission, I would like to submit my written testimony into the record.

Mr. SMITH. Without objection, so ordered.

Mr. MESERVEY. I need to add that the views I express in this testimony are my own and should not be construed as representing any official position of the Heritage Foundation.

Mr. Chairman, in the last two decades, China has built, by many measures, unparalleled influence in Africa. It has done so through an array of economic, military, and diplomatic initiatives.

Beijing wants to secure a stable supply of natural resources and make money in Africa. Yet, it is also seeking influence on the continent to support its rise to what it sees as its rightful place as a global superpower.

The U.S. prefers cooperation to competition, but the U.S. and Chinese models are fundamentally at odds, and the danger for U.S. interests is if the illiberal economic and governance model the Chinese exemplify continues to gain ground in Africa.

If it does, it would likely mean that U.S. and other countries' firms would be increasingly cut out of some of the growing economic opportunities on the continent, that the U.S.' longstanding foreign policy goal of encouraging the global growth of democracy would be turned back in Africa in favor of Beijing's authoritarian model, and that China could supplant the U.S. in strategic areas of the continent.

There are troubling signs that the Chinese model is gaining in Africa. Researchers found that as African countries' trade increases with China, they grow more likely to vote with Beijing against U.N. resolutions condemning human rights violations.

Polls show that while the U.S. as a model of national development holds a slight lead over China in Africa, China is even in southern and north Africa and leads in central Africa.

I want now to focus on a few of the ways China is building such influence. One part of Beijing's huge increase in economic activity in Africa has been issuing loans, as we have already been discussing this morning.

In 2015, Chinese loans from the 3 years previous accounted for an estimated one-third of all recent debt in sub-Saharan Africa. This gives it significant influence with many countries.

Djibouti, as we have also already been talking about, sits on the Bab-el-Mandeb Strait, a global shipping choke point. It hosts a number of military bases, including China's first permanent overseas base, and the U.S.' Camp Lemonnier.

China now holds Djiboutian debt worth about 60 percent of that country's GDP, giving it significant leverage over a country critical to U.S. military operations on the continent.

The Chinese base will supposedly serve as a rest and resupply depot for its forces participating in anti-piracy patrols and support Chinese personnel serving in U.N. peacekeeping operations in Africa.

The number of that personnel has skyrocketed to nearly 2,200 from only 20 in the '90s. China has recently enhanced other elements of its longstanding military ties with Africa.

From 2012 to 2015, Beijing accounted for nearly one-third of the value of all arms deliveries to the continent. Today, two-thirds of African countries use some Chinese military equipment. In addition, China trains militaries and builds military training centers in various African countries.

Across Africa, Beijing is also establishing Confucius Institutes, which are centers devoted to teaching Chinese culture and tradition, as well as pushing Beijing's narrative on topics such as Tibet and Taiwan.

Senior Chinese officials have described these institutes as important to Beijing's efforts to promote a positive Chinese global image, thereby strengthening Chinese national power.

In just over 10 years, the Chinese Government has established 76 Confucius Institutes and classrooms in 38 African countries.

Beijing is also training in China an increasing number of African politicians. These trainings sometimes cover decidedly illiberal topics such as how to control public opinion.

Other public diplomacy initiatives include Chinese medical teams conducting hundreds of African missions since 1963, and a hospital ship visiting at least nine African countries since 2010.

Some of Beijing's activities can be beneficial, such as filling part of Africa's huge infrastructure gap. Yet the U.S. should vigorously expand its own still significant influence in Africa to ensure the commitment to the rule of law, individual rights, and the free market is preeminent on the continent.

To do so, the U.S. should, among other initiatives, reorient its development aid to Africa to focus on enhancing free markets and accountable and competent governance, deepen cooperation with like-minded allies active on the continent such as the U.K., Israel, and Japan, swiftly fill the vacant Africa-related positions in the U.S. Government, and finally, seek opportunities such as in counterterrorism to cooperate with the Chinese while maintaining an appropriate level of wariness.

Thank you again for the opportunity to speak. I look forward to your questions.

[The prepared statement of Mr. Meservey follows:]

The
Heritage Foundation

CONGRESSIONAL TESTIMONY

China in Africa: The New Colonialism?

Testimony before the
Subcommittee on Africa, Global Health, Global Human Rights, and
International Organizations
United States House of Representatives

March 7, 2018

Joshua Meservey
Senior Policy Analyst, Africa and the Middle East
The Heritage Foundation

Chairman Smith, Ranking Member Bass, and members of the committee, thank you for this opportunity to testify before you. Thank you as well for highlighting one of the most important issues facing Africa, and by extension, U.S. interests on the continent, today. With your permission, I would like to submit my written testimony into the record.

My name is Joshua Meservey. I am the Senior Policy Analyst for Africa and the Middle East at The Heritage Foundation. The views I express in this testimony are my own and should not be construed as representing any official position of The Heritage Foundation.

China's Historic Engagements in Africa and Current Dominance

Even before many African countries gained independence, Chinese leader Mao Tse-tung recognized in the mid-1950s the continent's potential as a significant source of support for China's ambitions. His primary concern was to gain African states' diplomatic help to win from the rival Nationalist government in Taiwan global recognition as the mainland's official government, and to position China as the leader of the developing world in opposition to "imperialist" countries such as the U.S. and USSR.[1]

It was not until the turn of the 21ST century, after President Jiang Zemin called for China to "Go Out" to secure the resources and diplomatic support it needed to fuel its rise, that the pace and scale of Chinese engagements with Africa exploded. By many measures, China has been so active in going out that it is now the most influential foreign actor on the continent.

In 1992, China supplied just 1.8 percent of African imports. [2] Today, Chinese trade

---

[1] U.S. Central Intelligence Agency, "China's Role in Africa: Special Report Weekly Review," Washington, D.C.: GPO, February 25, 1972, https://www.cia.gov/library/readingroom/docs/CIA-RDP08S02113R000100080001-0.pdf.

[2] Lily Kuo, "The best days of selling cheap Chinese goods in Africa are over," *Quartz*, May 3, 2017,

volumes with Africa are three times larger than the continent's trade with India, its second-largest trade partner.[3] China is now the greatest source of imports for 19 of sub-Saharan Africa's 48 countries, up from being the largest import source for only 1 sub-Saharan African country in 2001.[4]

Beijing now also supplies Africa with more financing than any other country.[5] Chinese lending to the continent is opaque, but one of the best estimates is that Chinese government, banks, and contractors offered around $85 billion in loans to African governments and State-Owned Enterprises (SOEs) from 2000 to 2014, though only just over half were disbursed.[6] These loans are concentrated in a handful of countries, with five receiving more than half of them.[7] The transportation sector receives the most Chinese financing, followed by energy and mining and oil projects. [8] Infrastructure

development within those sectors is a priority, making Beijing the world's leading financier of African infrastructure.[9]

Chinese Foreign Direct Investment (FDI) in Africa is similarly difficult to gauge, but by one measure it has grown 40 percent annually for the last ten years from $1 billion in 2004 to $34 billion in 2015.[10] For the year 2016, China was by far the biggest foreign direct investor in Africa in terms of total dollars spent. China invested about 10 times what the U.S. did,[11] though the U.S.'s FDI stocks in Africa remain significantly higher than China's. While Chinese FDI targets virtually every part of the continent, about half of it is concentrated in eight countries.[12] The mining sector was the most popular destination for Chinese FDI in 2015, followed by construction and manufacturing.[13]

---

https://qz.com/950377/the-best-days-of-selling-cheap-chinese-goods-in-africa-are-over/.
[3] Irene Yuan Sun, Kartik Jayaram, and Omid Kassiri, "Dance of the Lions and Dragons," McKinsey & Company, https://www.africa-newsroom.com/files/download/aa9f2979a3dc18e.
[4] Daniel F. Runde and Christopher Metzger, "Is the United States Prepared for China to be Africa's Main Business Partner?," Center for Strategic and International Studies, January 31, 2018, https://www.csis.org/analysis/united-states-prepared-china-be-africas-main-business-partner.
[5] China appears to wish to continue to do so into the future. A senior official at the Export-Import Bank of China Bank recently estimated that China will provide $1 trillion in financing to African countries by 2025. Toh Han Shih, "China to Provide Africa with US$1tr Financing," *South China Morning Post*, November 8, 2013, http://www.scmp.com/business/banking-finance/article/1358902/china-provide-africa-us1tr-financing.
[6] Jyhjong Hwang, Deborah Brautigam, and Janet Eom, "How Chinese Money is Transforming Africa: It's Not What You Think," China-Africa Research Initiative at Johns Hopkins SAIS *Policy Brief* No. 11, April 2016, https://static1.squarespace.com/static/5652847de

4b033f56d2bdc29/t/5768ae3b6a4963a2b8cac955/1466478245951/CARI_PolicyBrief_11_2016.pdf.
[7] They are Angola, Ethiopia, Sudan, Kenya, and DRC. Hwang, et al. "How Chinese Money is Transforming Africa: It's Not What You Think."
[8] Deborah Brautigam and Jyhjong Hwang, "Eastern Promises: New Data on Chinese Loans in Africa, 2000-2014," China-Africa Research Initiative at Johns Hopkins SAIS, *Working Paper* No.4, April 2016, https://static1.squarespace.com/static/5652847de4b033f56d2bdc29/t/58ac91ede6f2e1f64a20d11a/1487704559189/eastern+promises+v4.pdf.
[9] Sun, et al., "Dance of the Lions and Dragons."
[10] Ibid.
[11] "Michael Lalor, et al., "Connectivity redefined," EY's Attractiveness Program Africa, May 2017, http://www.ey.com/Publication/vwLUAssets/ey-africa-attractiveness-report/$FILE/ey-africa-attractiveness-report.pdf.
[12] Angola, Cote d'Ivoire, Ethiopia, Kenya, Nigeria, South Africa, Tanzania, and Zambia. Sun, et al., "Dance of the Lions and Dragons."
[13] Janet Eom, et al., "The United States and China in Africa: What Does the Data Say?," China-Africa Research Initiative at Johns Hopkins SAIS *Policy Brief* No. 18, April 2017, https://static1.squarespace.com/static/5652847de

Private Chinese companies are increasingly important in Africa as well. There may now be as many as 10,000 Chinese owned firms on the continent, 90 percent of which are likely privately-owned.[14] This is in keeping with a trend that saw the private sector's share of all outward-bound Chinese investment rise from less than 10 percent in 2010 to nearly 50 percent in 2016.[15]

In keeping with the "Go Out" philosophy, about a third of all Chinese loans in Africa go to natural resource projects, [16] and more than 80 percent of China's Africa imports are of natural resources, including crude oil.[17] Oil-rich Angola is in fact the largest African recipient of Chinese loans.[18]

Beijing also targets relatively resource-poor but strategically important countries. Ethiopia—Africa's second most populous country and one of the world's fastest growing economies—receives the second-most Chinese loans to Africa.[19] China funds about 40 percent of the major infrastructure projects in Djibouti, [20] which has few resources but is one of the most strategically located countries in Africa. It sits on the Bab el Mandeb Strait through which about 50 percent of China's oil imports travel,[21] and hosts a number of foreign military bases, including the U.S.'s only permanent African military base.

China recognizes the many opportunities to make money in Africa as well. Huawei earns 15 percent of its global revenues on the continent,[22] and more than half of Chinese firms in a survey reported making back their initial investments in Africa in three years or less. [23] Beijing's frequent practice of providing "tied" loans [24] —resulting in as many as 70 percent of contracts for Chinese-financed projects going to Chinese companies [25] —has helped Chinese firms earn around $50 billion a year on African infrastructure projects alone. [26] These projects also help China's massive state-

---

4b033f56d2bdc29/t/58fd32a5ff7c502a493d18ed/
1492988584819/PB18_US+China+Africa.pdf.
[14]Sun, et al., "Dance of the Lions and Dragons."
[15]Derek Scissors, "Record Chinese Outward Investment 2016," American Enterprise Institute, January 2017, http://www.aei.org/wp-content/uploads/2017/01/China-Tracker-January-2017.pdf.
[16]"Chinese Loans to Africa Credit Limit," *The Economist*, April 30, 2016, https://www.economist.com/news/finance-and-economics/21697856-new-data-suggest-china-lends-less-africa-commonly-assumed-credit.
[17]Clara Sanna, "A Strategic Continent: China vs. Africa/The Atlantic Council's J. Peter Pham weighs in," *World Energy* No. 37, December 2017. https://www.aboutenergy.com/en_IT/flip-tabloid/oil_37_EN/index.html#slide24.
[18] Hwang, et al. "How Chinese Money is Transforming Africa: It's Not What You Think."
[19]Hwang, et al. "How Chinese Money is Transforming Africa: It's Not What You Think."
[20]Erica Downs, Jeffrey Becker, Patrick deGategno, "China's Military Support Facility in Djibouti: The Economic and Security Dimensions of China's First Overseas Base," CNA China Studies, July 2017,

https://www.cna.org/CNA_files/PDF/DIM-2017-U-015308-Final2.pdf.
[21]Andrew Jacobs and Jane Perlez, "U.S. Wary of its New Neighbor in Djibouti: A Chinese Naval Base," *New York Times*, February 25, 2017, https://www.nytimes.com/2017/02/25/world/africa/us-djibouti-chinese-naval-base.html.
[22]David Pilling, "Chinese investment in Africa: Beijing's testing ground," *Financial Times*, June 13, 2017, https://www.ft.com/content/0f534aa4-4549-11e7-8519-9f94ee97d996.
[23]Sun, et al., "Dance of the Lions and Dragons."
[24]Brook Larmer, "Is China the World's New Colonial Power?," May 2, 2017, *New York Times*, https://www.nytimes.com/2017/05/02/magazine/is-china-the-worlds-new-colonial-power.html.
[25]Yun Sun, "China's Aid to Africa: Monster or Messiah?," Brookings, February 7, 2014, https://www.brookings.edu/opinions/chinas-aid-to-africa-monster-or-messiah/.
[26]Andrew Jacobs, "Joyous Africans Take to the Rails, With China's Help," *New York Times*, February 7, 2017,

https://www.nytimes.com/2017/02/07/world/africa/africa-china-train.html.

owned infrastructure development companies offload some of the excess capacity they developed while building China's own infrastructure.[27]

Not all of Beijing's economic plays on the continent are designed to make money. The Chinese government is willing to support economically risky projects if they advance its foreign policy goals,[28] one reason Chinese SOEs on average earn lower profits than their private counterparts.[29] China's first major infrastructure project in Africa was the construction of the Tanzania-Zambia Railway, completed in 1976 and financed with a zero-interest Chinese loan, despite China suffering in the throes of the Cultural Revolution at the time.[30]

A Great Power's Soft Power
Current Chinese President Xi Jinping's "Chinese Dream" strategy envisions his country's return to what he sees as its rightful place of prominence on the global stage. Doing so requires, in addition to expanding its economic engagements at breakneck speed, enhancing a diverse range of public diplomacy initiatives.

A pillar of this effort has been the Chinese government controlled and funded Confucius Institutes. First established in Seoul, South Korea in 2004,[31] Confucius Institutes are designed to build sympathy and support for Beijing's geopolitical goals by promoting a positive image of China through exposure to Chinese culture and tradition, especially Mandarin language learning.[32] The institutes also push Beijing's narrative on controversial topics such as Tibet and Taiwan. In just over 10 years, the Chinese government established 48 Confucius Institutes and 28 Classrooms in 38 African countries.[33]

---

[27]For mention of the excess capacity, see William T. Wilson, "Is the Chinese Model Past Its Expiration Date?," in *2017 Global Agenda for Economic Freedom*, James M. Roberts and William T. Wilson, eds., The Heritage Foundation *Special Report* No. 188, https://www.heritage.org/international-economies/report/2017-global-agenda-economic-freedom.

[28]U.S. Central Intelligence Agency, "China's Role in Africa: Special Report Weekly Review."

[29]Sun, et al., "Dance of the Lions and Dragons." and Scissors, "Record Chinese Outward Investment 2016."

[30]Sun, "China's Aid to Africa: Monster or Messiah?"

[31]Claire van den Heever, "Inside Africa's Confucius Institutes," *WhoKou*, December 4, 2017, https://whokou.com/2017/12/04/inside-africas-confucius-institutes/.

[32] The Chinese government has been explicit about using Confucius Institutes to disseminate Chinese propaganda. Politburo member Li Changchun in 2011 said, "The Confucius Institute is an appealing brand for expanding our culture abroad. It has made an important contribution toward improving our soft power. The 'Confucius' brand has a natural attractiveness. Using the excuse of teaching Chinese language, everything looks reasonable and logical." In 2010, Chinese Minister of Propaganda Liu Yunshan wrote "With regard to key issues that influence our sovereignty and safety, we should actively carry out international propaganda battles against issuers such as Tibet, Xinjiang, Taiwan, human rights and Falun Gong... We should do well in establishing and operating overseas cultural centers and Confucius Institutes." Ethan Epstein, "How China Infiltrated U.S. Classrooms," *Politico Magazine*, January 16, 2018, https://www.politico.com/magazine/story/2018/0 1/16/how-china-infiltrated-us-classrooms-216327. National People's Congress member Hu Youqing stated, "Promoting the use of Chinese among overseas people has gone beyond purely cultural issues... It can help build up our national strength and should be taken as a way to develop our country's soft power." R.S. Zaharna, Jennifer Hubbert, and Falk Hartig, Confucius Institutes and the Globalization of China's Soft Power, (Los Angeles, CA: Figueroa Press, September 2014), http://uscpublicdiplomacy.org/sites/uscpublicdiplo macy.org/files/useruploads/u25044/Confucius%20 Institutes%20v2%20%281%29.pdf.

[33]Some estimate there are institutes in more than 40 African countries. van den Heever, "Inside Africa's Confucius Institutes." For the Chinese government's list of Institutes and Classrooms in Africa, see "Confucius Institute/Classroom."

Hanban, a branch of the Chinese Ministry of Education and the headquarters for the Confucius Institutes, offers scholarships to African students to study in China as well. Hanban scholarships have contributed to the number of African students studying in China growing 26 fold in 12 years. There are now more African students in China than in the U.S.—only France hosts more than China does.[34]

Echoes of Mao's shrewd practice of building influence with rising African leaders and political parties[35] remain today in Beijing's program for granting young—and sometimes senior—African politicians scholarships to attend trainings in China. Representatives of at least seven ruling parties in Africa have participated in the program,[36] and in 2016, China announced it would invite 1,000 more African politicians

to receive training.[37] Such initiatives give Beijing significant influence with officials who are likely to be part of their country's leadership in the future.

In 1963, Beijing opened a new soft power front in Africa by sending a medical team to Algeria. The teams, composed of doctors, nurses, and other medical personnel,[38] deploy for up to two years at a time, and are recruited by Chinese provincial-level governments. Provinces send teams to the same African country, thereby establishing a sustained "buddy system."[39] From 2000 to 2013, Chinese medical teams performed 189 missions to Africa.[40] China's Peace Ark hospital ship complements these efforts, and has visited at least nine African countries since 2010.[41]

Some Chinese firms are even beginning to launch the sort of image softening exercises

---

http://english.hanban.org/node_10971.htm. Institutes cater to university students, while classrooms are for students in the kindergarten to 12th grades.

[34]Victoria Moore and Nathan Breeze, "China Tops US and UK as Destination for Anglophone African Students," *The Conversation,* June 27, 2017, https://theconversation.com/china-tops-us-and-uk-as-destination-for-anglophone-african-students-78967.

[35]Mao supported with weapons and training a number of rebel groups—which later became ruling parties—battling for independence, including the African National Congress in South Africa, the South West African People's Organisation in Namibia, the Mozambique Liberation Front in Mozambique, and Robert Mugabe's Zimbabwe African National Union in Zimbabwe.

[36]They are the Ethiopian People's Revolutionary Democratic Front of Ethiopia; the National Congress Party of Sudan; Chama Cha Mapinduzi of Tanzania; South West African People's Organisation of Namibia; Sudan People's Liberation Movement of South Sudan; ANC and Communist Party of South Africa; and the Jubilee Party of Kenya.

[37]Lily Kuo, "Beijing is cultivating the next generation of African elites by training them in China, *Quartz,* December 14, 2017,

https://qz.com/1119447/china-is-training-africas-next-generation-of-leaders/.

[38]Tang Jailei and Xiao Bing, "China Has Medical Aid Teams Stationed in 42 African Countries," The China Africa Project, August 9, 2013, http://www.chinaafricaproject.com/china-has-medical-aid-teams-stationed-in-42-african-countries-translation/.

[39]Xiaoxiao Jiang Kwete, "Chinese Medical Teams in the DRC: A Comparative Case Study," China-Africa Research Initiative at Johns Hopkins SAIS *Policy Brief* No. 21, October 2017, https://static1.squarespace.com/static/5652847de4b033f56d2bdc29/t/5a26a4778165f5f17490c671/1512481911253/xiaoxiao+v9.pdf.

[40]Mohon Shajalal, et al., "China's engagement with development assistance for health in Africa," *Global Health Research and Policy* 2:24 (2017), August 9, 2017, https://ghrp.biomedcentral.com/track/pdf/10.1186/s41256-017-0045-8?site=ghrp.biomedcentral.com, 1-9.

[41]"Chinese hospital ship Peace Ark set out for 'Harmonious Mission – 2015'," *China Military Online,* September 25, 2015, http://english.chinamil.com.cn/news-channels/china-military-news/2015-09/25/content_6699367.htm.

more commonly associated with Western firms. In projects in Namibia and Kenya, Chinese firms made concessions to protect local wildlife.[42] Huawei is keen to be seen training 12,000 students a year in various countries, while a Chinese company in Namibia took the unprecedented step of inviting a labor union to organize at one of its mines.[43]

Projecting Global Military Force

Beijing appears to understand that achieving its desired status as a true global power requires projecting military force abroad. It has accordingly significantly strengthened its longstanding military ties with Africa. From 2012-2015, China accounted for more than 32% of the value of all arms deliveries to the continent, more than double the value of what it supplied from 2008 to 2011.[44] Today, two-thirds of African countries use some Chinese military equipment.[45]

China's military efforts in Africa increasingly feature boots on the ground as well. In 2017, China opened its first permanent overseas military base in Djibouti. Beijing claims the base will primarily be a rest and resupply depot for its forces participating in the multinational anti-piracy patrols off the East African coast that the Chinese joined in January 2009. The base will also support Chinese personnel serving in U.N. peacekeeping operations in Africa,[46] whose numbers have skyrocketed in the last two decades.[47] In addition, China is training militaries in a number of African countries, including Namibia and the Democratic Republic of Congo, and recently inaugurated a military training center the Chinese army built in Tanzania.[48]

Different Kinds of Strings

China frequently portrays its engagements in Africa as "no-strings-attached." It claims it does not meddle in the internal affairs of African countries, and makes no human rights, governance, or other demands. It is one of the central narratives it pushes with its African partners.[49]

The idea that there are no strings attached to Chinese engagement is an obvious canard, however. Some of the strings are simply different from those associated with other international partners, and have significant long-term costs.

African countries are increasingly saddling themselves with Chinese debt. From 2013 to 2015, Chinese institutions issued loans valuing $5 billion to $6 billion every year to African governments, constituting an

---

[42]David Pilling and Emily Feng, "Kenya's $4bn Railway Gains Traction from Chinese Policy Ambitions," *Financial Times*, April 4, 2017, https://www.ft.com/content/d0fd50ee-1549-11e7-80f4-13e067d5072c and Larmer, "Is China the World's New Colonial Power?"

[43]Larmer, "Is China the World's New Colonial Power?"

[44]Catherine A. Theohary, "Conventional Arms Transfers to Developing Nations, 2008-2015," Congressional Research Service, December 19, 2016, https://fas.org/sgp/crs/weapons/R44716.pdf.

[45]Ashley Cowburn, "Two-thirds of African countries now using Chinese military equipment, report reveals," *Independent*, March 1, 2016, http://www.independent.co.uk/news/world/africa /two-thirds-of-african-countries-now-using-chinese-military-equipment-a6905286.html.

[46]Jacobs and Perlez, "U.S. Wary of its New Neighbor in Djibouti: A Chinese Naval Base."

[47]"Troop and Police Contributors," United Nations Peacekeeping, https://peacekeeping.un.org/en/troop-and-police-contributors.

[48]"Here We Come, New Centre Warns Criminals," *Daily News*, February 7, 2018, https://www.dailynews.co.tz/index.php/home-news/55812-here-we-come-new-centre-warns-criminals.

[49]Larmer, "Is China the World's New Colonial Power?"

estimated one-third of all new debt in sub-Saharan Africa in 2015.[50]

In addition, about one-third of Chin's loans to African countries are collateralized with natural resources. [51] For some financially unstable countries with natural resources, commodities backed loans are the only option for securing financing—China financed the building of parts of its own infrastructure using this model.[52] However, if countries do not wisely negotiate the terms of these loans, a downturn in demand can leave them in economic distress. After oil prices began slumping in 2014, Angola was forced to send an increasing amount of oil to China to service its debt, leaving little for itself to sell to obtain much-needed cash.[53] Since 2004, China has struck at least 7 such deals with African countries.[54]

A default may even result in a country surrendering control or access to strategic assets, as happened recently when the Sri Lankan government gave up majority control of its Hambantota port to Chinese firms.[55]

African leaders are ultimately to blame for striking disadvantageous deals with the Chinese. However, Beijing sometimes, to gain control of a strategic asset or build political leverage, supplies loans to financially unstable countries with few other financing options.[56] It is also plausible that some Chinese lenders may offer African leaders personal financial inducements to borrow on terms favorable to Chinese interests. China has offered to cancel some African debt, but only small amounts.[57]

There is also the issue of reciprocity. China has snapped up African assets and rapidly increased its exports to the continent, but has been unwilling to fully open its own markets.[58]

China's extensive engagement in Africa also makes African governments and industries vulnerable to the sorts of economic, diplomatic, and military espionage China uses in other parts of the world. Beijing is the world's foremost perpetrator of economic espionage, and even institutionalized the practice in 1986 when

---

[50]Sun, et al., "Dance of the Lions and Dragons."
[51]Brautigam and Hwang, "Eastern Promises: New Data on Chinese Loans in Africa, 2000-2014."
[52]Deborah Brautigam, "China: Eastern Hope in Africa," *Observe*, August 25, 2011, http://www.observe-china.com/article/51.
[53]Libby George, "Growing Chinese Debt Leaves Angola with Little Spare Oil," *Reuters*, March 14, 2016, https://www.reuters.com/article/angola-oil-finance/growing-chinese-debt-leaves-angola-with-little-spare-oil-idUSL5N16H3EV.
[54]Brautigam, "China: Eastern Hope in Africa."
[55]Kiran Stacey, "China signs 99-year lease on Sri Lanka's Hambantota Port," *Financial Times*, December 11, 2017, https://www.ft.com/content/e150ef0c-de37-11e7-a8a4-0a1e63a52f9c and Ronak Gopaldas, "Lessons from Sri Lanka on China's 'debt-trap diplomacy'," Institute for Security Studies, February 21, 2018,

https://issafrica.org/iss-today/lessons-from-sri-lanka-on-chinas-debt-trap-diplomacy.
[56]Stacey, "China signs 99-year lease on Sri Lanka's Hambantota Port."
[57]Janet Eom, Jyhjong Hwang, Ying Xia, and Deborah Brautigam, "Looking Back and Moving Forward: an Analysis of China-Africa Economic Trends and the Outcomes of the 2015 Forum on China Africa Cooperation," China-Africa Research Initiative at Johns Hopkins SAIS *Policy Brief* No. 09, January 2016, http://static1.squarespace.com/static/5652847de4b033f56d2bdc29/t/56aa3a95a12f44bc3732d26e/1453996965486/CARI_PolicyBrief_9_Jan2016.
[58]Scissors, "Record Chinese Outward Investment 2016." Kenyan President Uhuru Kenyatta recently addressed the problem publicly, warning that "China must also open up to Africa." Pilling, "Chinese investment in Africa: Beijing's testing ground."

it launched Project 863 to facilitate the theft of U.S. trade and technology secrets.[59]

The fact that most Chinese companies operating in Africa are private only slightly ameliorates the risk, as even truly independent private Chinese firms would likely have to acquiesce if their government demanded they cooperate in some way. Some private firms are already significantly under the Chinese government's sway. There is currently a bill before the U.S. congress that would forbid the U.S. government from using products from Chinese telecommunications firms Huawei and ZTE. This follows multiple U.S. government reports finding that both companies pose a security risk because of their close ties to the Chinese government.[60]

The risk for African governments is significant. Huawei and ZTE have likely built more than 40 telecom networks in over 30 African countries, and national and government networks in more than 20 African countries.[61] According to the former head of the American NSA and CIA, Huawei shared with Beijing what it knows about Huawei-built foreign telecoms networks,[62] so it is likely that the Chinese government has already taken advantage of this African vulnerability.

A recent high-profile incident illustrates the problem. The African Union (AU) allegedly discovered that the servers in its Chinese-built headquarters in Addis Ababa were automatically uploading their contents every day to servers in China. A subsequent sweep of the building found numerous bugging devices. It is a likely sign of how strong Chinese influence on the continent has grown that the reaction from the AU and members states was muted. A number of African leaders, including Chairperson of the African Union Commission Moussa Faki Mahamat, even rejected the bugging reports as false.[63]

Part of what makes China so attractive is the one stop shop nature of some of their large projects, particularly infrastructure. Yet these package deals sometimes include anti-competitive requirements that result in governments not receiving as much value from the project as they should. Uganda's recently constructed Entebbe-Kampala road, for instance, cost twice as much to build per kilometer as did the Addis-Adama Expressway in Ethiopia, built by the same company. In order to secure a $350 million loan for their road from China's Exim bank, Uganda had to agree to single-sourcing,[64] a common Chinese lending requirement.

---

[59]"Foreign Spies Stealing US Economic Secrets in Cyberspace," Office of the National Counterintelligence Executive, October 2011, https://www.dni.gov/files/documents/Newsroom/Reports%20and%20Pubs/20111103_report_fecie.pdf.

[60]H.R. 4747, 115th Congress 2d Session, U.S. House of Representatives, January 9, 2018, https://www.congress.gov/115/bills/hr4747/BILLS-115hr4747ih.pdf.

[61]Andrea Marshall, "China's mighty Telecom footprint in Africa," New Security Learning, February 14, 2011, http://www.newsecuritylearning.com/index.php/archive/75-chinas-mighty-telecom-footprint-in-africa.

[62]"Former CIA boss says aware of evidence Huawei spying for China," Reuters, https://www.reuters.com/article/us-huawei-security/former-cia-boss-says-aware-of-evidence-huawei-spying-for-china-idUSBRE96I06I20130719.

[63]Ben Blanchard, "African Union Says Has No Secret Dossiers After China Spying Report," Reuters, February 8, 2018, https://www.reuters.com/article/us-china-africanunion/african-union-says-has-no-secret-dossiers-after-china-spying-report-idUSKBN1FS19W.

[64]Elias Biryabarema, "Chinese-built expressway divides Uganda as debts mount," Reuters, January 31, 2018, https://www.reuters.com/article/us-

Related to this is the issue of corruption. China is 77th of 180 countries ranked in Transparency International's most recent Corruption Perceptions Index, while sub-Saharan Africa is the worst performing region.[65] Unsurprisingly, 60 to 87 percent of recently surveyed Chinese firms in 5 African countries reported giving bribes to secure a license. [66] Just recently, the U.S. Justice Department charged an emissary of the private Chinese multinational, CEFC China Energy Company, with bribing Chadian and Ugandan officials in exchange for oil rights.[67]

Similarly, Beijing's training program for African politicians should worry any African who wishes for accountable governance. The Chinese Communist Party's (CCP's) recent decision to scrap presidential term limits is an illustration of the kind of model China is exemplifying for its African partners. Ethiopia's ruling party has learned about the Chinese government's techniques for controlling public opinion, including the media.[68] Part of the curriculum for South Africa's African National Congress and Kenya's Jubilee members concerned how to effectively organize and run a political party the way the CCP runs its affairs. In the case of Kenya, the program will include about 300 CCP officials traveling to Kenya to enhance the training.[69]

There are also environmental risks associated with China's burgeoning presence in Africa. Chinese nationals—and, allegedly, even Chinese diplomats[70]—are frequently important players in the poaching rings devastating Africa's wildlife. [71] An estimated 48 percent of exports of Mozambican timber to China is illegal. [72] China's massive, and heavily subsidized, fleet of fishing trawlers gets most of its distant-sea catch from West African waters. As many as two-thirds of those Chinese boats fish illegally, rapidly depleting fishing stocks and costing West Africa an estimated $2 billion a year.[73]

uganda-road/chinese-built-expressway-divides-uganda-as-debts-mount-idUSKBN1FK0V1.
[65]"Corruption Perceptions Index 2017,"
Transparency International, February 21, 2018,
https://www.transparency.org/news/feature/corruption_perceptions_index_2017#table.
[66]Sun, et al., "Dance of the Lions and Dragons."
[67]Alexandra Stevenson, "U.S. Bribery Case Sheds Light on Mysterious Chinese Company," *Financial Times*, November 21, 2017,
https://www.nytimes.com/2017/11/21/business/china-energy-cefc.html.
[68]Yun Sun, "Political party training: China's ideological push in Africa?," Brookings, July 5, 2016,
https://www.brookings.edu/blog/africa-in-focus/2016/07/05/political-party-training-chinas-ideological-push-in-africa/
[69]Ibid and Stephanie Findlay, "South Africa's Ruling ANC Looks to Learn from Chinese Communist Party," *Time*, November 24, 2014,
http://time.com/3601968/anc-south-africa-china-communist-party/F and Jeff Angote, "Jubilee looks to the Communist Party for lessons," *Daily Nation*, September 18, 2016,
http://www.nation.co.ke/news/politics/Jubilee-looks-to-the-Communist-Party-for-lessons/1064-3385490-yy2x8x/index.html.
[70]Benjamin Haas, "Under pressure: the story behind China's ivory ban," *The Guardian*, August 29, 2017,
https://www.theguardian.com/environment/2017/aug/29/story-behind-china-ivory-ban.
[71]Larmer, "Is China the World's New Colonial Power?" and "Vanishing Point: Criminality, Corruption and the Devastation of Tanzania's Elephants," Environmental Investigation Agency, November 2014, https://eia-international.org/wp-content/uploads/EIA-Vanishing-Point-lo-res1.pdf.
[72]"First Class Connections: Log Smuggling, Illegal Logging, and Corruption in Mozambique," Environmental Investigation Agency, February 2013, https://eia-international.org/wp-content/uploads/EIA-First-Class-Connections.pdf.
[73]Andrew Jacobs, "China's Appetite Pushes Fisheries to the Brink," *New York Times*, April 30, 2017,
https://www.nytimes.com/2017/04/30/world/asia/chinas-appetite-pushes-fisheries-to-the-brink.html.

The Stakes

There are positive elements to China's African engagements. Beijing is helping close Africa's huge infrastructure gap that is a serious drag on economic growth. China is supporting secure maritime shipping, a global good, through its participation in anti-piracy patrols. Chinese firms supply African consumers with affordable products. Despite the predatory nature of some Chinese loans, responsible African countries could benefit from Chinese lending as well.

Africa also has enough economic opportunities to go around. The Chinese dominate construction and claim a growing share of the continent's nascent manufacturing sector, but the U.S. has a competitive advantage in increasingly important sectors such as financial services and agribusiness.[74]

Yet China's rise in Africa presents a number of challenges to the U.S. In many African countries, the norms and regulatory environments around governance and economic activity are still forming. Countries like China that are not committed to equitable and transparent economic competition are influencing those norms, disadvantaging U.S. and other countries' firms. African countries will also not reap as much advantage as they would in a fair economic system.

Furthermore, the U.S. for decades has encouraged the global growth of democracy, both because it is the political system best able to promote human flourishing, and because democratic countries are likelier to support U.S. foreign policy goals. The authoritarian governance model the Chinese exemplify for African leaders is antagonistic to that objective.

Finally, there is danger that China will use its influence on the continent to supplant American influence, as it is seeking to do in the Indo-Pacific region. [75] As just one example of the potential risks for the U.S., Beijing holds Djiboutian debt worth about 60 percent of the country's gross domestic product,[76] giving it significant leverage over a country critical to U.S. military operations in Africa.

The stakes in this contest are immense. By 2030, one estimate projects 19 African economies will be growing by 5 percent or more per year, and that the continent will constitute a $3 trillion economy. [77] The African Development Bank predicts that household expenditures in Africa will grow to $3.5 trillion in the following eight years.

Africa is also home to extraordinary natural resource wealth. The continent has 60 percent of the world's uncultivated arable land, approximately 7.5 percent of the world's known oil and gas reserves, and an estimated 30 percent of the world's mineral reserves. Those reserves include 12 of the 23 minerals the U.S. deems critical to its economy and national defense, and for

[74]Aubrey Hruby, "Escaping China's Shadow: Finding America's Competitive Edge in Africa," Atlantic Council's Africa Center *Issue Brief,* September 2017, http://www.atlanticcouncil.org/publications/issue-briefs/escaping-china-shadow.
[75]Admiral Harry B. Harris Jr., "U.S. Pacific Command Posture," testimony before the House Armed Services Committee, U.S. House of Representatives, February 14, 2018, https://armedservices.house.gov/legislation/hearings/military-and-security-challenges-and-posture-indo-pacific-region.
[76]Jacobs and Perlez, "U.S. Wary of its New Neighbor in Djibouti: A Chinese Naval Base."
[77]Lalor, et al., "Connectivity redefined."

which the U.S. is more than 50 percent import reliant.[78]

The continent is also strategically positioned. It touches three of the world's eight maritime chokepoints,[79] abuts Europe and Asia, and has thousands of miles of Atlantic and Indian Ocean coastline. Recognizing the continent's strategic importance, a host of countries are ramping up their activities in Africa.[80]

African countries as well remain an important force in international diplomacy, as Mao recognized back in the 1950s. In 1956, Egypt was the first African country to recognize Mao's regime, followed by 14 others in the next 9 years.[81] In 1971, 26 African countries helped Beijing win the U.N. seat held by Taiwan at the time.[82] Since 2005, China has persuaded 5 of the 7 African countries that maintained diplomatic relations with Taiwan to break them. [83] African countries also comprise the largest geographically based voting bloc in many international fora, and frequently vote together.

China appears to be gaining in the battle to influence African norms. According to the latest polling, the U.S. as a model of national developments holds a slight lead over China, but the latter is even in Southern and North Africa, and leads in Central Africa.[84] Sixty-three percent of polled Africans had a mostly positive view of China's influence,[85]

---

[78]The U.S. is currently significantly dependent on China for importation of at least 9 of those 23 critical mineral commodities. China now dominates the global supply chain for cobalt—necessary for making lithium-ion batteries which will likely be critical to powering self-driving cars, a potentially massive industry in the near future—50 percent of which is produced in the Democratic Republic of Congo. Scott Patterson and Russell Gold, "There's a Global Race to Control Batteries—and China Is Winning," *Wall Street Journal*, February 11, 2018, https://www.wsj.com/articles/theres-a-global-race-to-control-batteriesand-china-is-winning-1518374815?mod=e2tw. The 12 critical mineral commodities found in Africa are Antimony, Barite, Cobalt, Graphite, Lithium, Manganese, Niobium, Platinum, Rare Earths, Tantalum, Tin, and Titanium Mineral Concentrate. "Critical mineral resources of the United States—Economic and environmental geology and prospects for future supply," Klaus J. Schulz, et al., eds., U.S. Geological Survey *Professional Paper* 1802, https://minerals.usgs.gov/minerals/pubs/mcs/2017/mcs2017.pdf and "Mineral Commodity Summaries 2017," U.S. Department of the Interior and U.S. Geological Survey, 2017, https://pubs.er.usgs.gov/publication/pp1802A.
[79]Rob Bailey and Laura Wellesley, "Chokepoints and Vulnerabilities in Global Food Trade," Chatham House, June 2017, https://www.chathamhouse.org/sites/files/chathamhouse/publications/research/2017-06-27-chokepoints-vulnerabilities-global-food-trade-bailey-wellesley-final.pdf.
[80]Joshua Meservey, "The Saudi-Qatari Dispute: Why the U.S. Must Prevent Spillover into East Africa," The Heritage Foundation *Backgrounder* No. 3268, https://www.heritage.org/global-politics/report/the-saudi-qatari-dispute-why-the-us-must-prevent-spillover-east-africa.
[81] U.S. Central Intelligence Agency, "China's Role in Africa: Special Report Weekly Review."
[82]Sun, et al., "Dance of the Lions and Dragons."
[83]Burkina Faso and Swaziland maintain relations with Taiwan, despite lavish Chinese offers of aid. Pauline Bax, Simon Gongo, and Lungile Dlamini, "Chinese Billions Fail to Sway Taiwan's Last Two Allies in Africa," Bloomberg, January 24, 2017, https://www.bloomberg.com/news/articles/2017-01-24/chinese-billions-fail-to-sway-taiwan-s-last-two-allies-in-africa and Raymond W. Copson, Kerry Dumbaugh, and Michelle Lau, "China and Sub-Saharan Africa," Congressional Research Service, August 29, 2005, https://www.everycrsreport.com/files/20050829_RL33055_8a2febe8cfa3f6075443ada838ab5667422215d2.pdf.
[84]"China's growing presence in Africa wins largely positive popular reviews," Afrobarometer *Dispatch* No. 122, October 24, 2016, http://afrobarometer.org/sites/default/files/publications/Dispatches/ab_r6_dispatchno122_perceptions_of_china_in_africa1.pdf.
[85]Ibid.

and China's global popularity is greatest in Africa.[86]

China Plans a Future in Africa, but There Are Challenges

The U.S. will have to grapple with the reality of China as a major force in Africa for the foreseeable future. More than 40 percent of Chinese firms surveyed in Africa reported making long-term investments in the continent, and nearly three quarters were bullish on future opportunities.[87]

Furthermore, while Chinese firms do benefit from Beijing's practice of privileging them on Chinese-financed projects, they also win so much African business because they have developing world experience from building large infrastructure projects in their own country. The Chinese also offer "one stop shop" package deals on infrastructure that often include financing, construction, and maintenance. Chinese firms also are known for making quick decisions, and then rapidly delivering. Finally, they frequently come in at a significantly lower price than competitors.[88] These practices will keep them competitive in Africa.

Yet it is unclear how sustainable China's habit of giving easy loans to unsuitable countries is. Africa's debt problem is so severe—more than half of sub-Saharan African countries have debt levels greater than 50 percent of GDP, up from 11 in 2013[89]—that it is virtually certain that some of China's African debtors are going to default or have to renegotiate the repayment terms. Beijing may have to

reassess whether the influence, or even the strategic assets or commodities, it gains from such arrangements are worth the expense.

One of China's advantages in Africa is that its firms have a higher risk tolerance than most. Yet that also means that Beijing will have to increasingly grapple with how to respond when upheaval strikes some of these unstable countries in which Beijing has significant interests. The Chinese navy had to evacuate thousands of Chinese nationals from Libya in 2011, after that country descended into civil war. The current tumult gripping Ethiopia, a key Chinese partner,[90] the recent succession struggle in Zimbabwe, and the ongoing civil war in South Sudan are other examples of tests for the Chinese. This is a strain on Beijing's decision makers, and any decisive action they take risks undermining its important non-interventionist narrative on the continent.

Furthermore, the Chinese economy has a number of long-term challenges, including capital flight, unsustainable debt levels, and all the inefficiencies associated with planned economies.[91] If the Chinese economy slows, Beijing may come under domestic pressure to curtail some of its lavish overseas spending to concentrate on problems at home.

---

[86]Pilling, "Chinese investment in Africa: Beijing's testing ground."

[87]Sun, et al., "Dance of the Lions and Dragons."

[88]Ibid.

[89]Brahima S. Coulibaly and Christian Golubski, eds., "Foresight Africa: Top Priorities for the Continent in 2018," Brookings, https://www.brookings.edu/wp-content/uploads/2018/01/foresight-2018_full_web_final2.pdf.

[90]Ethiopia receives the second most Chinese loans to Africa, and more than two-thirds of surveyed Chinese firms in the country have made long-term investments there. Ibid.

[91]Wilson, "Is the Chinese Model Past Its Expiration Date?"

Finally, some African countries may be starting to experience the downsides of engaging with China. Kenya is struggling to convince importers to use its recently constructed, $4.2 billion standard gauge railway, 90 percent of which was financed by China's Eximbank.[92] Chinese loans have also been hotly debated in countries such as Ghana and the Democratic Republic of Congo, with opposition parties in particular urging renegotiation.

The Way Ahead

The U.S. response to China's rising influence in Africa should not be to demonize Beijing, but rather to coordinate its various elements of influence to promote the U.S. model as a positive alternative. The U.S. has a number of advantages on which to build in Africa: it is generally well liked and admired, has decades-long military, economic, and diplomatic ties with many African countries, and gave the continent nearly $10 billion in overseas development assistance in 2016 alone.

The U.S. should:

- Increase its engagement with Africa, and reorient the focus of some existing initiatives. Such measures should include focusing the U.S.'s overseas development assistance on enhancing countries' free market systems and encouraging accountable and competent governance; enhance the efficiency of U.S. aid by eliminating "buy American" provisions and subsidies to U.S. shipping companies that deliver aid; boosting trade beyond the African Growth and Opportunity Act; and making the U.S.-Africa Leaders Summit a regular event.[93]

- Confidently advocate for American values with the African public and its leaders. Most people yearn for representative government, rule of law, and individual freedom, and the U.S. should take every opportunity to communicate how its system promotes those values. U.S. officials should also quietly remind America's African friends that Chinese engagement has a number of significant costs that do not come with a U.S. partnership.

- Prioritize the fight against African corruption, not least because it is a significant Chinese competitive advantage. Ideas for doing so include helping countries strengthen their civil societies, promoting economic freedom, leveraging technology and the power of crowds, and elevating the fight against graft as part of U.S. development assistance.[94]

- Encourage countries borrowing from the Chinese to make the process as transparent as possible.

- Swiftly fill the vacant Africa-related positions in the U.S. government, particularly the Assistant Secretary of State for African Affairs position and ambassadorial posts in key countries such as South Africa.

[92]Macharia Kamau, "State Offers More Incentives to Woo Cargo Owners to Use SGR," *Standard Digital*, March 3, 2018, https://www.standardmedia.co.ke/business/article/2001271779/state-offers-more-incentives-to-woo-importers-to-use-sgr and Pilling and Feng, "Kenya's $4bn Railway Gains Traction from Chinese Policy Ambitions."

[93]Joshua Meservey, "Africa," The Heritage Foundation's *Solutions 2018*, 2018, https://solutions.heritage.org/restoring-american-leadership/africa/.

[94]Joshua Meservey, "The Impact of Corruption on Economic Development in sub-Saharan Africa" in *2017 Global Agenda for Economic Freedom*, James M. Roberts and William T. Wilson, eds., The Heritage Foundation *Special Report* No. 188, https://www.heritage.org/international-economies/report/2017-global-agenda-economic-freedom.

- Deepen cooperation with like-minded allies operating on the continent. A number of American allies, such as Israel, Germany, the U.K., and Japan, are active on the continent, and their interests frequently align with those of the U.S.
- Cooperate with China where possible. There are areas where the U.S. can cooperate with Beijing, such as in counterterrorism. As many as 5,000 Uighurs from China have traveled to Syria to fight.[95] As China's international footprint expands, its people and infrastructure will grow increasingly vulnerable to attacks, and the U.S. has a national interest in fighting terrorism wherever it appears.

Thank you again for this opportunity to testify, and I look forward to any questions you may have.

* * * * * * * * * * * * * * * * * *

---

[95]Gerry Shih, "AP Exclusive: Uighurs fighting in Syria take aim at China," *Associated Press*, December 23, 2017, https://apnews.com/79d6a427b26f4eeab2265719 56dd256e/AP-Exclusive:-Anger-with-China-drives-Uighurs-to-Syria-fight. This number is disputed. For a lower estimate, see Bassem Mroue and Gerry Shih, "Chinese jihadis' rise in Syria raises concerns at home," *Associated Press*, April 22, 2017, https://www.apnews.com/591f9b238c84477b87cf ac68bfe169fc.

Mr. SMITH. Thank you so very much for your testimony and I look forward to the questions because I do have a number—a few, as well.

I'd like to now yield to Mr. Morris.

STATEMENT OF MR. SCOTT MORRIS, SENIOR FELLOW, CENTER FOR GLOBAL DEVELOPMENT

Mr. MORRIS. Mr. Chairman, Ranking Member Bass, thank you for the opportunity to testify, even at the last minute. I appreciate it very much.

I'd like to use my time to highlight some new research from me and my colleagues at the Center for Global Development, John Hurley and Gailyn Portelance, on the question of China's lending practices and their implications for debt distress in developing countries. I'll also offer some of my personal views on the implications of this research for U.S. policy.

Our new work, which I've submitted to the committee along with my testimony, specifically looks at the debt implications of China's belt-and-road initiative.

While much of the initiative falls outside of Africa, we do identify a handful of African countries as part of belt-and-road. We also look broadly at Chinese practices associated with debt distress, which has particular relevance for African countries.

We find that Chinese lending could lead to debt distress in at least eight countries associated with belt-and-road due to the current debt profile of those countries, the volume of Chinese lending contemplated under the initiative, and the predominantly commercial terms of that lending.

Djibouti, which we have already heard a lot about, is one of the most vulnerable of these countries. It is the site of China's only overseas military base and has been the recipient of large-scale Chinese lending and investment.

Our analysis suggests that Djibouti's external debt, already very high for a low-income country, could rise to over 90 percent of GDP under the belt-and-road lending.

Equally important, nearly all of this external debt—over 90 percent—will be owed to China. So if Djibouti faces a debt crisis, how is China likely to respond? The answer is we don't know, which speaks to why Chinese practice in this area is problematic.

China's approach to debt relief isn't particularly transparent or predictable, yet transparency and predictability are critical to managing debt problems in an orderly way.

This is why the work of the Paris Club of Creditors, which includes the United States along with other major creditor countries, rests on well-articulated rules and actions pursued on a collective basis.

China is not a member of the Paris Club and has only participated in the club's agreements on a very limited basis.

So what does all this mean for the United States? First, even as we highlight Chinese practices that are clearly problematic in the developing world, we also should acknowledge that degree to which Chinese financing is contributing and helping to spur growth in these economies.

Ethiopia is a case where we see a mix of Chinese projects and investments, some that may not be sustainable or productive alongside others that are clearly delivering an economic benefit to the country.

So as long as this is the case, as it very well may be in a wide range of countries, then dire warnings from the United States are unlikely to find a receptive audience in the developing world.

Instead, we should be specific in our criticism of Chinese lending practices and look for specific opportunities to engage the Chinese on reform.

We would do well to continue to press the Chinese on alignment with global norms and practices on lending transparency, debt management, procurement standards, et cetera.

Progress is frustratingly slow but it's not entirely absent. As a member of the G-20, China has signed on to important principles around sustainable financing which includes commitments to lending transparency.

U.S. officials should aim to steer these G-20 commitments to operational practice. We should also prioritize our own engagement in the developing world. This means continuing to exercise leadership in the humanitarian and health sectors as well as beefing up our development finance tools.

On the latter, the proposed U.S. Development Finance Corporation for which there is legislation now would mark a positive step forward, I think.

At the same time, we should be realistic about its utility as an answer to China. It is not likely to operate on a scale that rivals Chinese development finance institutions, and as private sector focus, while important, also limits its role in purely public infrastructure.

Fortunately, we do have a ready-made set of tools in our toolkit when it comes to deploying high-quality development finance across Africa and globally.

U.S. leadership in institutions like the World Bank and the African Development Bank is of critical value and I worry that current policy fails to exploit the full potential of these institutions.

These banks define best practice in the very areas that concern us about Chinese lending, from setting appropriate lending terms to ensuring open and transparent procurement rules.

If we are worried about China's growing presence in a wide array of countries globally, then now is not the time to be shrinking the footprint of these institutions.

So, rather than resisting the World Bank's call for more capital this year, I would suggest that U.S. officials take whatever the number that the bank has requested and double it, and then repeat this exercise across all of the multilateral development banks.

This certainly may sound overly ambitious, but would only account for just a few more percentage points of our foreign aid budget.

Whether or not we can muster this level of ambition it will be critical for U.S. policy to be defined by a positive agenda in the developing world. It is a losing proposition to limit ourselves to the role of China's chief critic if we have nothing to offer in the alternative.

Thank you.
[The prepared statement of Mr. Morris follows:]

Testimony of

Scott A. Morris

Senior Fellow, Center for Global Development

Before the

Committee on Foreign Affairs

Subcommittee on Africa, Global Health, Global Human Rights, and International Organizations

Hearing on "China in Africa: The New Colonialism?"

2:00 p.m., Wednesday, March 7, 2018

Mr. Chairman, Ranking Member Bass,

Thank you for the opportunity to testify this afternoon. I would like to use my time to highlight some new research from me and my colleagues at the Center for Global Development, John Hurley and Gailyn Portelance, on the question of China's lending practices and their implications for debt distress in developing countries. I will also offer my personal views on the implications of this research for US policy.

Our new work, which I have submitted to the committee along with this testimony, specifically looks at the debt implications of China's Belt & Road initiative. While much of the initiative falls outside of Africa, we do identify a handful of African countries as part of Belt & Road. We also look broadly at Chinese practices associated with debt distress, which has particular relevance for African countries.

We find that Chinese lending could lead to debt distress in eight countries associated with Belt & Road due to the current debt profile of those countries, the volume of Chinese lending contemplated under the initiative, and the predominately commercial terms of that lending.

Djibouti is one of the most vulnerable of these countries. It is the site of China's only overseas military base and has been the recipient of large-scale Chinese lending and investment. Our analysis suggests that Djibouti's external debt, already very high for a low-income country, could rise to over 90 percent of GDP under Belt & Road lending. Equally important, nearly all of this external debt (over 90 percent) will be owed to China.

So if Djibouti faces a debt crisis, how is China likely to respond? The answer is we don't know, which speaks to why Chinese practice in this area is problematic. China's approach to debt relief isn't particularly transparent or predictable. Yet, transparency and predictability are critical to managing debt problems in an orderly way. This is why the work of the Paris Club of creditors, which includes the United States along with other major creditor countries, rests on well-articulated rules and actions pursued on a collective basis. China is not a member of the Paris Club and has only participated in Paris Club agreements on a very limited basis.

So what does all of this mean for the United States? First, even as we highlight Chinese practices that are clearly problematic in the developing world, we also should acknowledge the degree to which Chinese financing is spurring growth in these economies. Ethiopia is a case where we see a mix of Chinese projects and investments—some that may not be sustainable or productive alongside others that are clearly delivering an economic benefit to the country. So long as this is the case, as it very well may be in a wide range of countries, then dire warnings from the United States are unlikely to find receptive audiences in the developing world.

Instead, we should be specific in our criticism of Chinese lending practices and look for specific opportunities to engage the Chinese on reform. We would do well to continue to press the Chinese on alignment with global norms and practices on lending transparency, debt management, procurement standards, etc. Progress is frustratingly slow, but it's not entirely absent. As a member of the G20, China has signed onto important principles around sustainable financing, which include commitments to lending transparency. US officials should aim to steer these G20 commitments to operational practice.

We should also prioritize our own engagement in the developing world. This means continuing to exercise leadership in the humanitarian and health sectors, as well as beefing up our development finance tools. On the latter, the proposed US Development Finance Corporation would mark a positive step forward. At the same time, we should be realistic about its utility as an answer to China. It is not likely to operate on a scale that rivals the Chinese development finance institutions, and its private sector focus, while important, also limits its role in purely public infrastructure.

Fortunately, we do have a ready-made set of tools in our toolkit when it comes to deploying high quality development finance across Africa and globally. US leadership in institutions like the World Bank and African Development Bank is of critical value, and I worry that current policy fails to exploit the full potential of these institutions. These banks define best practice in the very areas that concern us about Chinese lending, from setting appropriate lending terms to ensuring open and transparent procurement rules. If we are worried about China's growing presence in a wide array of countries globally, then now is not the time to be shrinking the footprint of these institutions. So, rather than resisting the World Bank's call for more capital this year, I would suggest that US officials take whatever the number the bank has requested and double it. Then repeat that exercise across all of the multilateral development banks. This may sound overly ambitious, but it would account for just a few more percentage points of our foreign aid budget.

Whether or not we can muster that level of ambition, it will be critical for US policy to be defined by a positive agenda in the developing world. It is a losing proposition to limit ourselves to the role of China's chief critic if we have nothing to offer in the alternative. Thank you.

Mr. SMITH. Thank you so very much for your testimony and insights.

I'd like to now call on our final witness, Dr. Plummer.

STATEMENT OF ANITA PLUMMER, PH.D., ASSISTANT PROFESSOR, DEPARTMENT OF AFRICAN STUDIES, HOWARD UNIVERSITY

Ms. PLUMMER. Thank you, Chairman Smith and Ranking Member and the honorable members of this committee, Congressman Bera.

It is an honor to appear before you today to discuss China's engagement with Africa. I want to begin with a note that I think will contextualize my remarks.

Africa is a diverse continent with 54 countries which, except for Liberia and Ethiopia, share a legacy of colonialism which has shaped political, economic institutions, culture, and its position in the global system.

When discussing China's engagement with Africa, some generalizations may be appropriate, but to have substantive discussion, we should consider the features of the commitments on a case-by-case basis.

So in the spirit of specificity, I will focus my testimony on Kenya's ties with China to hopefully illustrate some of the nuances and ambiguities of China's role in Africa.

In 2008, the Kenyan Government implemented its Vision 2030 Development Program. The program's goal is to transform Kenya into a newly industrializing middle income country with far-reaching political, economic, and social reforms.

The government has undertaken a robust agenda that focuses on large-scale infrastructure. Coincidentally, China's belt-and-road initiative, a project aimed at developing overland and maritime trade routes connecting Asian, European, and African countries, corresponds with Kenya's goal to secure its role as a gateway to eastern and central Africa.

Kenya's geostrategic position provides much-desired access to consumer markets as well as the facilitation of extractive industries in South Sudan, Uganda, and the Eastern Democratic Republic of Congo.

Infrastructure is the third largest sector that the Chinese are engaged in on the continent of Africa following mining and financial services. On the macro level, the rationale is that investments in telecommunications, energy, and transport will increase foreign direct investment in the country and region.

On the micro level, there is an assumption that large-scale capital investments in infrastructure will promote economic growth by integrating rural areas with urban business centers.

For Kenya, investments in transport are viewed as an imperative because its landlocked neighbors, such as Tanzania, South Sudan, and Uganda rely on its road and rail network along with its ports in Mombasa and the one slated to be built in Lamu.

Conversely, the East Africa region, home to 230 million consumers, is an attractive destination for products, particularly from China.

Foreign direct investment by emerging economies such as China has been a vital part of Kenya's growth strategy. Kenyan policy makers believe that the delivery of mega transport projects will boost their competitiveness in the global market and increase possibilities for high-value production in different sectors.

However, China's engagement with Africa has included significant debt finance investments in transport infrastructure. This engagement brings inevitable conflicts between diverse actors from China and local Kenyan communities who must contend with the ambiguities of China's role in Africa and its implications for labor markets and sites of production.

Within the Kenyan context where exogenous factors have historically driven development, infrastructure delivery is a political process and in the absence of quality decision making that is participatory and transparent, government and business elites overlook criticisms of this model.

These critiques include those that you're well aware of—debt traps, environmental degradation, lack of skills transfer, and so on.

These projects are primarily financed by Chinese banks or institutions and its financing is tied to Chinese companies being awarded the contracts. African Government value turnkey projects and the accompanied funding.

African leaders applaud China's responsiveness to requests for development projects. The largest one in the country to date is the standard gauge railway.

However, in response to high rates of youth unemployment, particularly in Kenya, youth have protested for jobs, decent wages, safe working conditions, and environmental sustainability—all promises made by both Kenyan and Chinese Governments when the projects were announced.

Second, infrastructure projects aimed at supporting extractive industries or ensuring Chinese-made goods easily reach African markets is too narrow an approach to economic development.

It may be convenient to argue that China's presence is neocolonial. But that fails to consider African agency in determining the scope and scale of their relations with China.

China's strategy is rooted in its imperative to access resources in markets, to appear to be a global responsible power, and to isolate Taiwan's role in Africa.

Conversely, African leaders want to use China's presence in their nations to boost their political legitimacy both domestically and internationally. The issue at hand is how to assess the extent to which elites in Africa and China are fostering policies and practices that further extract from people's livelihoods and constrict political space.

A dangerous trend that we do not want to see in African nations follows what we have observed in China with Xi Jinping's efficient consolidation of power. Currently, there is a problem with the lack of transparency in Sino-African engagements which results in mutually reinforcing practices among African and Chinese elites of acting autonomously from their citizens, and this is despite a robust campaign of public diplomacy in Africa by Chinese diplomats who frame China as nonpaternalistic and nonhegemonic.

I want to add that there is also discussion in Africa on the implications of China's role in hindering the democratic project and how shifts in U.S. policy may further undermine grassroots efforts to promote African democracy.

For example, in an op-ed published yesterday in one of Kenya's most widely-read papers, the author, Wachira Maina, wrote, "China does not have a democracy agenda. Its investments in Africa and its flexible apolitical diplomacy have allowed its clients to resist the political terms that the West wants imposed for aid on the continent."

He goes on to write, "Fearing that it could lose out if it stuck to ethical foreign policy in the face of Chinese incursion, the West has changed its posture. Western diplomats now talk stability, not democracy. Elections are okay if they are peaceful rather than free and fair. Quiet diplomacy is increasingly favored over visible, public, and the frank approach of the 1990s. With China in the foreground, the West bargains from a weak position."

In conclusion, the model of political authoritarianism and economic liberalism is appealing to most African leaders. But African publics interpret this model differently.

The assumption made by elites in China and Africa is that liberal economic frameworks are the most efficient tool for development and their investments in large-scale transport energy infrastructure support that view.

The other assumption made by the leadership in China and Africa is that institutions built on democratic norms are inefficient and antithetical to growth.

As the U.S. considers its engagement in Africa in an increasingly crowded political and business environment, i.e., China, India, and Brazil, it may consider shifting attention to supporting development from within. That is supporting efforts to create space for African-based entrepreneurs to flourish and for civil society to continue to push for political pluralism and inclusivity.

Thank you.

[The prepared statement of Ms. Plummer follows:]

Anita Plummer, Ph.D
Assistant Professor, Howard University
Committee on Foreign Affairs
Subcommittee on Africa, Global Health, Global Human Rights and International Organizations
March 7, 2018
"China in Africa: The New Colonialism?"

Thank you to Chairman Smith and Ranking Member Bass and the honorable members of this committee. It is an honor to appear before you today to discuss China's engagement with Africa. I want to begin with a note that I think will contextualize my remarks. Africa is a diverse continent with fifty-four countries (except for Liberia and Ethiopia) that share a legacy of colonialism which has shaped political and economic institutions, culture and its position in the global system. When discussing China's engagement with Africa, some generalizations may be appropriate, but to have a substantive discussion, we should consider the features of the commitments on a case by case basis. In the spirit of specificity, I will focus my testimony on Kenya's ties with China to hopefully illustrate some of the nuances and ambiguities of China's role in Africa.

In 2008, the Kenyan government implemented its Vision 2030 development program. The program's goal was to transform Kenya into a newly industrializing, middle-income country with far-reaching political, economic, and social reforms. The Vision 2030 Delivery Secretariat, the body responsible for administering the development policy, has undertaken a robust agenda that focuses on large-scale infrastructure. Simultaneously, China's Belt and Road initiative, a project aimed at developing overland and maritime trade routes connecting Asian, European, and African countries correspond with Kenya's goal to secure its role as the gateway to Eastern and Central Africa. Kenya's geostrategic position provides much-desired access to consumer markets as well as the facilitation of extractive industries in South Sudan, Uganda, and eastern Democratic Republic of Congo, DRC. Both Vision 2030 and the Belt and Road initiative call for substantial investments in Africa's transport sectors. Infrastructure is the third largest sector that the Chinese are engaged in on the continent of Africa after mining and financial services. On the macro-level, the rationale is that investments in telecommunications, energy, and transport will increase foreign direct investment in the country and the region. On the micro-level, there is an assumption that large-scale capital investments in infrastructure will promote economic growth by integrating rural areas with urban business centers. For Kenya, investments in transport are viewed as an imperative, because its landlocked neighbors such as Tanzania, South Sudan, and Uganda rely on its road and rail network, along with the ports in Mombasa and the one slated to be built in Lamu. Conversely, the East Africa region, home to 230 million consumers, is an attractive destination for products, particularly from China.

Foreign direct investment by emerging economies such as China has been a vital part of Kenya's growth strategy. Kenyan policymakers believe that that the delivery of mega transport projects will boost their competitiveness on the global market and increase the possibilities for high-value production in different sectors. China's engagement with Africa has included significant debt-financed investments in transport infrastructure. This engagement brings inevitable conflicts between diverse actors from China and local Kenyan communities, who must contend with the ambiguities of China's role in Africa and its implications for labor markets and production.

Within the Kenyan context, where exogenous factors have historically driven development, infrastructure delivery is a political process, and in the absence of quality decision-making that is participatory and transparent, government and business elites overlook counter-channels of discourse that provide a nuanced critique of the outcome of exogenously-led infrastructure.

First, these projects are primarily financed by Chinese banks or institutions and financing is tied to Chinese companies being awarded the contracts. African governments value turnkey projects and the accompanied funding. China's physical presence building roads, railways, dams, and pipelines provide a sense of tangible progress. African leaders applaud China's responsiveness to requests for development projects. However, in response to high rates of youth unemployment, particularly in Kenya, youth have protested for jobs, decent wages, safe working conditions, and environmental sustainability—all promises made by both the Kenyan and Chinese governments when projects were announced. Second, infrastructure investments aimed at supporting extractive industries or ensuring that Chinese-made goods easily reach African markets is too narrow an approach to economic development.

It may be convenient to argue that China's presence is neocolonial, but that fails to consider African agency in determining the scope and scale of their relations with China. China's strategy is rooted in its imperative to access resources and markets and to appear to be a responsible global power. Conversely, African leaders want to use China's presence in their nations to boost their political legitimacy both domestically and internationally. The issue at hand is how to assess the extent to which elites in Africa and China are fostering policies and practices that further extract from people's livelihoods and constrict political space. A dangerous trend that we do not want to see in African nations follows what we have observed in China with the Xi Jiping's efficient consolidation of power. Currently, there is a problem with a lack of transparency in Sino-African engagements which results in a mutually reinforcing practice among African and Chinese elites of acting autonomously from their citizens. This is despite, a robust campaign of public diplomacy in Africa by Chinese diplomats who frame China as a non-paternalistic and non-hegemonic partner in Africa.

In conclusion, the model of political authoritarianism and economic liberalism is appealing to African leaders, but African publics interpret this model differently. The assumption made by some elites in China and Africa is that liberal economic frameworks are the most efficient tool for development and investments in large-scale infrastructure support that view. The other assumption is that institutions built on democratic norms are inefficient and antithetical to growth. As the U.S. considers its engagement in Africa in an increasingly crowded political and business environment (i.e., China, India, Brazil) it may consider shifting attention to supporting development from within. That is, supporting efforts to create space for African based entrepreneurs to flourish and for civil society to continue to push for political pluralism and inclusivity.

46

Mr. SMITH. Thank you very much, Dr. Plummer.

To begin the questioning, let me begin by asking Mr. Chang and any others who would like to jump in on these questions, in your testimony—first of all, let me just preface that.

I do co-chair the China Commission with Marco Rubio. We had another hearing just a few days ago on Tibet and the tightening noose on the Tibetan people under Xi Jinping, which has been bad, but is getting worse.

He does the same thing with the Christian churches, the Falun Gong, religious groups of all kinds, the Uighurs, as well as with NGOs, which now have a very much tightened space within which to operate, all under Xi Jinping.

Our annual report, which we put out every year—it's a bipartisan report—nine members of the House, nine members of the Senate, and five of the executive branch—was the most scathing we have ever had since the inception of the China Commission, again, underscoring that Xi Jinping is truly in a race to the bottom with North Korea when it comes to human rights.

Why is that important, of course? Because their model which they are seeking to export, and until recently—until the changes— hoped for changes in Zimbabwe, you know, they got along very well with Robert Mugabe and others like him, but not so with more democratically-elected African countries.

So my first questions would be about this threat to good governance. Do you see it? You've all spoken about the debt.

I remember, when George W. Bush, and Bono, and others in this Congress, in a bipartisan way, we all worked to try to help highly-indebted countries get out from under through debt relief, and it continued for many, many years.

But it seems like that may be turning a corner, and as was pointed out in testimony today, the connection of those debts or those loans, I should say, to extractive industries and the like and projects is very, very high.

So the first question would be, do the Chinese pay a fair price to Chinese companies or government companies in China for the products that they sell, whether it be minerals, oil, or whatever it might be?

Is there a longer-term cost that's not immediately apparent? The debt-forgiveness—when does that reach a critical mass?

Is it approaching that in terms of loan sharks—you know, it's over time that it becomes more troubling, and if there are all kinds of strings attached and, as was said during today's testimony by Mr. Meservey, the no-strings-attached approach applies to a lot of things, especially to human rights and good governance issues— Tibet, Taiwan.

Mr. Chang, you made several very, very powerful statements that the dealings between Beijing and African states seem to be tainted by both corruption and several forms of coercion.

You might want to elaborate on that, if you would. You also pointed out that China is spreading its economic and political model to Africa.

There are some people who thought at the beginning—not me and probably not anybody at this table—that it was not a package deal—that the bad governance model follows it. And you also made a point that Xi Jinping's ambitions are beyond helping the developing world.

There are indications that he, in fact, wants China's model to be the world's model, and that the Chinese leader should be the world's leader, and you point out that Xi suggested the world would be peaceful should Beijing rule it as an "all-under-Heaven approach," obviously, using their words.

They use the word "Tianxia." Could you explain that further? I've done a lot of reading about the Japanese. My father fought in New Guinea and the Philippines. He was a combat infantryman.

So that issue of the Japanese—the why of it has always fascinated me, troubled me like it does so many. The Japanese have this idea called "the eight corners of the world under one roof," which wasn't just imperial Japan—it predated that—that they had this almost divine right to encircle the Earth with their ideology and their governance. It was one of the reasons—maybe the reason—for their aggression against, first, Asia, and then, elsewhere.

The comparisons, if there are any, with China today may not be religiously based. They are not claiming Hirohito to be divine. They are not saying Xi Jinping is divine. But they seem to have an ideology that says they are destined to rule the world.

And I look everywhere, from Europe to Latin America. This subcommittee deals with human rights all over the world, and the Chinese influence is profound. Again, it's no strings attached. So I wonder if you could speak to that possible connection, or are there any comparisons there?

Mr. CHANG. Thank you, Chairman Smith.

One of the most striking elements of Xi Jinping, in addition to the consolidation of power that Dr. Plummer talked about, really has been his ambitions for China.

And in this, he's been using language recently that indicates that he believes that China should be the world's only sovereign—a proposition which sounds ludicrous but nonetheless we have to look at what he's actually been saying.

So over the course of a decade he's been using language of "all under Heaven," which is the concept that China's emperors for two millennia used.

We saw some of these in some of the words that were used during the slogans for the 2008 Summer Olympics. This became very clear in his 2017 New Year's message where he talked about the world being all under Heaven, would be happy if we were one family.

And then, if all of this weren't clear enough, in September of last year, Wang Yi, the foreign minister of China, published an article in Study Times, which is the paper of the Communist Party's Central Party School, and in that article Wang Yi says that Xi Jinping Thought—that's a body of work—the way the Chinese refer to an ideology—that Xi Jinping Thought transcends and replaces 300 years of Western thinking on international relations.

Well, if you go 300 years back, you're just about at 1648, which is the Treaty of Westphalia, which established the basis of the world's international system today of competing sovereign states.

So what you can look at in terms of the "Tianxia"—the "all under Heaven" language that Xi Jinping has been using—and looking at

Wang Yi's Study Times article, it's pretty clear the way the Chinese are looking at these things.

And, indeed, China's house scholars study this concept. Now, as I mentioned, this is breathtaking but this is what they are telling us.

Now, you know, in terms of comparisons with the Japanese, the Chinese don't have this notion of divinity as much as the Japanese do in the Shinto religion.

But nonetheless, you can see the idea that there is one power that's supposed to be in the world that will make the world peaceful and safe and that just happens to be Japan in the 1930s and China in our time.

And so we have to be—of course, there are differences. But when you combine this with China's views of Africans on a personal level, this becomes extremely dangerous.

Now, of course, you know, many African countries have benefitted from certain aspects of what China has done. But what we have also seen is China trying to use low-cost loans basically to encourage governments to spend freely, to create the crises of the future—these debt crises.

We have these in a number of countries that were mentioned so far and, indeed, at this very moment Tanzania is trying to restructure its debt and having discussions with Beijing and with multilateral institutions in China—to a certain extent, is undermining what those multilateral institutions are trying to do.

So when you put that together with the low-level corruption, sometimes high-level corruption, it's a very difficult picture for Africa and one which the United States needs to speak out about.

Mr. SMITH. You did, in your testimony—before we go to any other witnesses—talk about how China's words appear ominous and not benign and you used the words "colonial master."

You also pointed out, and as a matter of fact, Mr. Meservey pointed out the Confucius Institutes and how troubling they are, and the fact that so many African leaders are being brought to China for schooling just to train up the next generation of leaders—again, using the bad governance model.

And as far as I know, and maybe you can correct me if I am wrong, we have the Foreign Corrupt Practices Act, which tries to mitigate bribery and the like. Not so with China, as far as I know.

I've never seen anything that would even come close to suggesting they had such a thing. So if you could answer those. Then I'll yield to my good friend, Ms. Bass.

Mr. CHANG. The colonial master language is really the result of China trying to divest other nations of sovereignty because that is the essence of colonialism.

Today, you know, one can argue about the nature of China's relations with the countries on the continent and, of course, as Dr. Plummer has pointed out, those relations differ from country to country.

But we do see certain trends which concern us and we have talked about the debt, because through debt, China gains a hold over political systems in various countries.

You know, and we have seen this not just in Africa. This is something that they've done, for instance, on our own continent with

Venezuela—something that has a direct effect very close to our home—where China is now using the renegotiation process to gain advantage in our own continent. Of course, they do that in Africa as well.

One can argue that a country can do whatever it wants to gain power. But nonetheless, when we put all of these things together, it paints an extremely disturbing picture.

So we can't look at just low-cost loans in isolation. We can't look at just Xi Jinping's thoughts on the Treaty of Westphalia in isolation. We can't look at the corruption that China has fostered or the bad governance that it tends to promote.

You put all of that together and the picture is one of danger not only for Africans but for others as well.

Mr. MESERVEY. Yes, I'll address a couple of those questions.

One is the fair price for resources that you referenced earlier and the answer is that we don't know because so frequently these arrangements are very opaque and that's one of the criticisms that you'll hear even among the African public or usually opposition politicians will make this point.

No one quite knows what China is paying for access to certain resources. But I—and even with some of the large infrastructure projects—we mentioned the standard gauge railway in China—in Kenya, excuse me—those too are starting to come under scrutiny.

There is growing concern I think in Kenya that the standard gauge railway is a white elephant. There was—there was three newspaper articles about this just earlier this week where they were concerned—the Kenyan Government trying to compel importers to use the standard gauge railway because they still didn't want to use it.

And, of course, the specter is looming that they are going to be stuck with an extraordinarily expensive piece of infrastructure that isn't going to return on—that isn't going to produce a return on investments.

There is also another example in Uganda where a road was built by the same Chinese company that built a road in—from Addis to Eritrea and the road in Kenya was twice the cost, essentially, than the one in Addis—from Addis to Eritrea.

And as I mentioned, it was built by the same company and part of the problem was the contract was—demanded single sourcing so meaning a Chinese company, which ended up being this company that had been involved in the Ethiopia projects got the contract and that's caused a lot of consternation—why, again, was this road in Uganda so much more expensive. So there is starting to be these questions asked not just about are African countries getting a fair price for their resources but also are they getting good value on these massive infrastructure projects.

Mr. MORRIS. Mr. Chairman, I wanted to address one question you raised around that forgiveness and you mentioned the heavily-indebted poor country initiative—HIPC—which, I have to say, the U.S. Congress really demonstrated tremendous leadership on for the international community at the time.

And I think it is instructive because if you look at what made HIPC work at the time, it had a lot to do with who these countries owed money to and it was essentially the World Bank, the IMF, and the G-7 and you had the possibility and the reality of those actors getting together and deciding to act in concert to relieve debt in the face of evidence that this was a tremendous burden on these poor countries mostly in Africa.

If you look at the profile of debt—of countries today that we are worrying about—again, many in Africa—it looks very different.

In fact, increasingly it is not the G-7 at all. They are simply not there as creditors. It is still the World Bank, the IMF, but it is China and then it is a set of other emerging actors.

And so far, we are not seeing any evidence that these actors and primarily the Chinese have an interest in engaging in this kind of collective engagement around considering debt relief.

It's not that the Chinese have not done debt relief. They do it on an ad hoc basis. Some ways—in some ways they do it in a very traditional way that looks like the way that the Paris Club might do it.

But then other times they do things that, frankly, look—let's call it peculiar—in terms of debt for equity swaps, debt for land swaps and it's that set of activities that really, you know, from my perspective, is a cause for concern and does worry me about, you know, the potential for wide-scale debt problems and what will the international community be able to do this time around, given the state of play compared to what it looked like 15 years ago.

Ms. BASS. Thank you. Thank you very much, Mr. Chairman.

One question I would like for all of you to address in a minute is what's the solution here because, to me, as Mr. Morris said, it's easy to sit here and be real critical of China. But what leverage do we have over China to get China to act differently?

And, you know, Mr. Morris, you were just talking about 15 years ago, and the role that the U.S. played, and it seemed as though— it seems as though maybe we have an opportunity to play that role again by mobilizing the international community.

It might not be that the debt is owed to the IMF and G-7. I believe you said it wasn't. But maybe the world community has leverage. Because I just don't understand what the solution is.

I mean, to me the solution is the U.S., and our stepping up. I don't know if you four have other ideas as to what the solution is.

But, you know, I could look at how the Chinese could easily say several things about our involvement, from the military to youth leaders to all of that, which I think our involvement is very positive, especially in terms of training the next generation of leaders.

But I am concerned about the lack of our involvement and the direction that we are going in terms of the cuts to the State Department and all of that.

But there is the independent private sector that I am hoping, and I am sure the chairman is, too, would step up more and be more involved in China's—I mean, in Africa's infrastructure.

So maybe each of you could tell me what the solution is that's different than the U.S. stepping up.

What leverage do we have to tell China to stop acting the way it's acting in the continent of Africa?

Mr. CHANG. Well, Ranking Member Bass, I think the United States has enormous leverage over China. We have a much bigger economy. We have a stable economy.

China right now is heading to a debt crisis and there are a number of different ways that we can deal with the Chinese. One of them is just a very simple one. We could enforce U.S. law against North Korean banks that are laundering—Chinese banks that are laundering money through New York on behalf of North Korea.

I mean, a threat to, for instance, declare the Bank of China a primary money laundering concern under Section 311 of the PATRIOT Act could rock the Chinese financial system.

Ms. BASS. Can we do that, Mr. Chairman? Sanction the Bank of China?

Mr. CHANG. I think that we can because there is evident proof that there is—Bank of China's involvement in, for instance, devising and operating a money laundering scheme for the North Koreans in Singapore.

This was in a U.N. panel of experts report for the year 2016. There is other evidence that the Bank of China has been involved in money laundering for the North Koreans in other locations, and the Bank of China, as big as it is, is not the biggest Chinese bank.

But the point is not so much—you know, this does not relate to Africa but we do have——

Ms. BASS. That is what I am referring to.

Mr. CHANG. Excuse me?

Ms. BASS. That is what I am referring to.

Mr. CHANG. Yes. We can do it. We have the authority to do it. Matter of fact, we should be doing it because we shouldn't allow anybody, especially Beijing, to use our financial system in ways that violate American law.

Ms. BASS. Okay.

Mr. CHANG. But to answer your question in terms of Africa, China's influence in Africa is largely because it's got these economic relationships, not only just extracting minerals but also selling goods in China—in Africa.

And we have a very different system. You know, our companies don't say yes when the President of the United States calls up. They very well can say no. But that's not the Chinese system. When you have a big Chinese enterprise or a big Chinese bank, they have to do what they are told by the party and——

Ms. BASS. Right. And I am not—and I am not doubting you. You know, that's fine. But my question was—and you answered it in part with the Bank of China. I don't think we are going to do that but you answered part of it.

What is the solution outside of us stepping up? And maybe I'll pass it on to Mr.——

Mr. CHANG. Just quickly.

Ms. BASS. Yes, go ahead.

Mr. CHANG. You know, I think democracy promotion that was very important——

Ms. BASS. That we cut. Go ahead.

Mr. CHANG. Also, our aid, for instance, is not building these big buildings, for instance, like the African Union headquarters, which was bugged by the Chinese.

But our aid has been more people-oriented. You know, it's developing in local communities—clean water, vaccines, all the rest of it.

Ms. BASS. Yes, and I have a problem with how we do our aid too because I don't think our aid promotes self-sufficiency of African countries that I believe have the capacity to do a lot of those things themselves.

Mr. CHANG. And we should be doing more of those things that do promote self-sufficiency because they are extremely popular among people and this is a struggle for hearts and minds.

So that's where I would concentrate our efforts and, of course, I think, you know, it's an all-of-the-above issue where, you know, if we should be putting more money into the IMF. Yes, let's do that. Let's do all of these things.

But I like the idea of essentially the way we work with countries, you know, at the local level because that's important for people-to-people relationships, and the Peace Corps is a very important initiative in that regard.

Mr. MESERVEY. Yes. I agree with your fundamental point that the best way to approach this challenge is to enhance American activities.

Ms. BASS. Pull your microphone up a little bit. It's hard to hear you.

Mr. MESERVEY. Oh, sorry. I agree with your fundamental point that the best way to deal with these—this challenge is to enhance American activity because we do still have immense influence on the continent.

We give—last year or in 2016, rather, we gave $10 billion in overseas development assistance to Africa. So that alone buys us immense leverage.

Now, I don't think we have used it as well as we should have.

Ms. BASS. Right.

Mr. MESERVEY. But to your—to your—the core of your question of what leverage do we have over China, we don't—so China cares deeply about its international image, for instance.

So I would point to the ivory ban that recently the Chinese Government implemented in China, and I think they became embarrassed about the fact that Chinese demand for ivory had been driving this poaching epidemic across the African continent. And so eventually they started to do something.

Now, whether they are going to continue, whether it is a truly good-faith effort, we will see. But at least, in my mind, it was an incremental step at the very least. So international image issues—there is a limit, too. If it—if it conflicts with their core interests they don't care how they look.

But so there is a limit to that. But that's something. Prosecuting corruption—there was, again, a recent case. The Department of Justice laid charges against an emissary from a major multinational Chinese company—a private company that had bribed Chadian officials and Ugandan officials, I think, for access to oil rights. So seizing those opportunities.

But, fundamentally, China in Africa is a fact of life and it will be for the foreseeable future. So and there are good elements to Chinese activity.

Now there are all these negative things that I think are best dealt with by enhancing our own activities, as you said in your opening remarks and in your questions, and just burnishing the attractiveness of the American model, which still has a lot of resonance on the continent.

Ms. BASS. Thank you.

Mr. MORRIS. Thank you, Congresswoman.

I would say what's critical and what I am worried about is that we are not maintaining the level of engagement directly with the Chinese that helps make progress on these issues and, as I said in my testimony, however painfully slow that might be, the absence of the engagement isn't going to—going to do anything positive.

And I would point to one example. So you have something called the Strategic Dialogue. It's changed names over the years. But it was started in the Bush administration, carried forward in the Obama administration.

And over the course of the years, it addressed many different issues, one of which was this issue about debt problems in low-income countries and China's behavior.

Just a few years ago, the signals were that China was very close to joining the Paris Club of Creditors, which I referred to in my testimony as a really important forum for dealing with debt problems and doing it in a responsible way.

What I see now is no evidence that that dialogue is a priority anymore for this administration and statements from Treasury officials that it simply isn't a priority. And, you know, from my perspective we probably lost an opportunity as a result to keep that momentum up on questions like responsible lending practices.

Ms. BASS. Thank you. Yes?

Ms. PLUMMER. Very thoughtful questions—one that I've been grappling with for years in terms of what we can do on our end.

One, in terms of leverage, the U.S. is still favored over China. So opinion polls that have taken place in nearly every sub-Saharan African country by the Pew, Global Attitudes Project, and Afrobarometer show that U.S. values are still favored over the values of authoritarian bureaucracy that are heralded from China.

So when we look at leverage, we have to look at it on the level of the elites that we are engaging with but also the masses of people who are impacted by our policies.

So initiatives, like the YALI initiative, I think are very encouraging to support young entrepreneurs, civil society leaders in developing strategies to be able to bring pressure on their governments from below.

I think we should also look at debt models and consider debt forgiveness. Billions of dollars are leaving the continent every year servicing debt——

Ms. BASS. Right.

Ms. PLUMMER [continuing]. But also linked to illicit financial flows. The U.S. has a very robust system and we can look at where African leaders are stashing billions of dollars offshore including in banks in the United States. I think——

Ms. BASS. And buying property here.

Ms. PLUMMER. And buying property here. This is money that belongs to the masses of African people. So in terms of U.S. leverage and building on the favorable image that the U.S. already has in Africa, I think it will be much welcomed if our policies really consider how the masses would be impacted by our policies.

Finally, I think the Millennium Challenge Corporation had a very good model in terms of money going to development projects in Africa being given to African companies to carry out the projects.

So expanding MCC, also considering expanding AGOA and preferential trade treatment. What products are given preferential treatment is also a very tangible area that the U.S. can improve its policy on.

Ms. BASS. Thank you.

And just to wrap up, Mr. Chair, I would agree with you in terms of the U.S. being valued over the Chinese because some of the roads we are talking about and infrastructure, we know, collapses.

But, you know, again, I think it falls on us. One of the other issues that I don't believe you raised, or maybe I missed the various panelists, is one of the problems is labor. So, you know, in communities in—well, my community, for example—part of my district's people get upset if there is a major project and no one on the project is from the community. I can only imagine what Africans feel who are unemployed and see Chinese labor come in.

All of those, to me, are reasons why I think we should focus on the U.S. and increase our footprint on the continent, and leave our viewpoint of the continent—our viewpoint of the continent is from a charity perspective—what you watch on late-night TV on Africa in terms of the commercials.

Until we leave that viewpoint and join the rest of the world in looking at the continent of Africa from the point of view of partnership and opportunity, and then promote U.S. businesses to do business on the continent. We can sit and complain about China all we want. But, to me, it's a question of us stepping up.

And with that, I yield back.

Mr. SMITH. Thank you.

Chairman Chabot.

Mr. CHABOT. Thank you very much, Mr. Chairman.

Last month, it was brought to my attention that the tribal rivalry between the Dinka and Nuer people in South Sudan has resurfaced.

I've heard reports that the Chinese Government is directly benefitting from this conflict by extracting resources with virtually no benefit for the people who inhabit the land and possibly even using enslaved locals for their labor.

Could any of you speak to this or have you heard of Chinese engaging in similar practices in other parts of Africa?

Mr. MESERVEY. I'll take a stab.

So I follow South Sudan quite closely and yes, the Chinese companies are heavily involved in that country, specifically in the oil industry, which is one of the areas of contestation in the country because, obviously, it's lucrative to control the oil fields.

Again, I don't know what the specific terms of the contract are because they are very rarely ever made public. So it's very difficult to know what are the Chinese paying and things of that nature.

But I suspect that in this case, given how thoroughly corrupt the South Sudanese regime is and how its primary concern is to prosecute the war in South Sudan, that it would happily strike a very poor deal with these Chinese companies in order to have some sort of—in order to earn some money at all because they are under very difficult financial strain.

To the question about slave labor, I haven't encountered or heard of that happening in South Sudan specifically.

But one of the concerns of Chinese engagement on the continent is the standards for labor, and frequently, they are not up to the standards that a Western firm would demand or uphold.

So I—and this has caused conflict in other parts of the continent where there have even been deaths when miners have struck, for instance, at Chinese mines and then been shot.

So I wouldn't at all be surprised if there are serious labor abuses in the South Sudanese oil fields as well.

Mr. CHABOT. Thank you very much.

Would any other panel members want to add anything to that? If not, I'll move to another question. Okay. I'll go ahead.

China is notorious for undermining Taiwan every chance it gets. I was one of the original founders of the Congressional Taiwan Caucus and have been working on Taiwan issues for many years now.

How has Beijing leveraged its influence in Africa against Taiwan? What impact has increasing Chinese influence in Africa had on Taiwan's global standing, for example, pressing countries across the globe including in Africa to drop their recognition of Taiwan? Would anybody want to address that?

I saw you nodding, Mr. Meservey. So if you'd like to——

Mr. MESERVEY. Sure. I address this in my written testimony.

In 2005, there were seven African countries that recognized Taiwan. There are two left now, and that's the result of a campaign by the Chinese on the continent.

Sao Tome and Principe was the most recent African country to cut ties. That was just last year—late last year—and they immediately received very large Chinese loans.

The Chinese have never given loans to countries that maintain ties with Taiwan. There are only two left, as I said—Burkina Faso and Swaziland.

And I suspect—I didn't go back before 2005 but if you went further back I am sure there were many more African countries with ties to Taiwan that have—that have steadily cut them off because of Beijing's inducements.

Mr. CHABOT. Thank you.

And then finally, when China builds good will when it does various projects in Africa but really around the world, it always does so with the expectation that its partner will disproportionately favor China.

There is always something in it much more for China. You might think you're getting something out of it and it's sort of free but it's never free with China.

I know you've all addressed this in your testimony. But to what extent will Chinese investment perhaps make various countries in Africa less hospitable to Western businesses and organizations because of the way they've undermined free and open markets, rule of law—the way you're actually supposed to do things?

Anybody is—Mr. Chang?

Mr. CHANG. Yes. I mean, that generally has been Beijing's ultimate intention.

You know, when Chinese companies first go to a country they can't do that. But what we have seen in Africa and elsewhere that when there is this critical mass that Beijing does have the ability to use its economic power for what you've mentioned—to undermine.

The whole concept of Beijing undermining good governance in Africa and elsewhere it's just been so clear and we have seen the effects of it in countries like Zimbabwe.

So with the big men in Africa, they do have Chinese support and that's sort of an indication where Beijing would go if it indeed had more influence.

Mr. CHABOT. Very good.

Thank you very much. I yield back, Mr. Chairman.

Mr. SMITH. Let me just ask a few followup questions or follow up on final questions, and thank you again for your very, very incisive answers.

Could any of you shed any light on what the relationship is between the Chinese Government and the African Union? What are their goals? What are they trying to influence, if anything, in your view, with the AU?

Ms. PLUMMER. So the Chinese Government built the African Union headquarters. So that's obvious.

It's interesting that the Chinese Government prefers not to engage in negotiations with blocs—power blocs. They prefer to negotiate on a bilateral basis, and that's obvious.

Any time a group of countries negotiate as a bloc, especially countries that aren't as integrated like in Africa, that will put China at a better advantage in terms of negotiating trade deals.

There are representatives from the Chinese Government at the African Union headquarters. Aside from that, I am not sure of how the Chinese Government uses the African Union to lobby African leadership or what access they have in the African Union because they have their Embassies in each country that they have ties with.

And I would imagine that on a bilateral basis within each country the relationships are stronger outside of the AU.

Mr. SMITH. Thank you.

Mr. Meservey, you pointed out in your testimony, and I quote, "Echoes of Mao's shrewd practice of building influence with rising African leaders and political parties remain today in Beijing's program for granting young and sometime senior African politicians scholarships to attend trainings in China."

You point out that in 2016 China announced it would invite 1,000 more African politicians to receive training.

Do you, or any of you, have any sense what that training actually is? What is the duration of it? You know, is it indoctrination all wedded together with what? Do we know?

Mr. MESERVEY. Like many elements of Chinese engagement with Africa, it's a bit opaque. But there is no doubt that some—and I reference this in the written testimony—some of these representatives of African political parties are receiving training on how the CCP organizes its own party, for instance.

The EPRDF, which is the ruling coalition in Ethiopia, which in your opening remarks you referenced its deeply authoritarian tendencies, has received trainings on how to control public opinion including relations with the media.

So I think the thrust of a lot of these trainings—and there is also—there are objectively benign trainings like around agricultural competencies and such—but the thrust for a lot of the parties—the African parties that are interested and I think there have been at least seven ruling African parties that have participated in these trainings—is learning how to—to learn how to sort of—learn how to dominate the country, frankly, as the CCP does and I think it's deeply worrying when you have parties like the Jubilee Party from Kenya.

Kenya is a democracy, but they are going to receive trainings—we don't know the content of all of them but we suspect that they are—the CCP is training parties like Jubilee and the EPRDF and SWAPO in how to deepen their own and centralize their authority.

Mr. SMITH. Yes, Mr. Morris.

Mr. MORRIS. Mr. Chairman, if I could, I think it's important that we not underestimate the degree to which China is becoming a desirable place to obtain technical knowledge.

Their increasingly sophisticated economy, investing heavily in areas of R and D, and to the degree that they are, you know, actively seeking to attract students from other countries, let's recognize that's our model and I do worry that at the moment that feels a little vulnerable here and I think it's one of the ways in which we have been so effective in the world is that we have been particularly open to foreign students who come to our universities.

And so that—you know, as a model that is now growing in China we need to recognize its value to us as well.

Mr. SMITH. But is there any kind of political baggage that goes along with that? Because we know for a fact that the Confucius Institutes and many of our colleges and universities who have campuses on mainland China are highly restricted in what they are able to do and that there is a political baggage weight that is imposed by having such an institute, for example, on a U.S. campus.

And we are looking further into it on the China Commission. Like I said before, we have asked the GAO to really vigorously study what the parameters are—what they are teaching—because, like I said in my opening remarks, it's like a free gift to a university to have what seems to be a value added, but really, in real terms, probably is not. It's soft power.

Mr. CHANG. Mr. Chairman, just on one aspect, I don't know the nature of the training that the Chinese are offering.

But the one big drawback that China suffers is that African students and others have been the targets of really ugly racism in China and that must have tarred the image.

And one of the great things about the United States is just the openness of it and so that when students come here they generally have a very positive view of the United States, and we have to work at that, of course.

But Beijing does suffer from it because it does have the money to bring everybody to Beijing but it doesn't have the ability to change Chinese attitudes and those attitudes, I think, are the biggest impediment to China making actually more inroads into the African societies.

Mr. SMITH. On one trip to the DR Congo I remember meeting with a group of lawmakers who told me that the Chinese are very adept at making sure that the roads go close to minerals and that which they have their eyes on, and often have access to it at a very small or negligible price. They also said the roads weren't that good.

What is your sense in terms of the quality of the goods? We know that, in Kenya, a bridge, several months ago, collapsed in Kenyatta. I had been there visiting just 2 weeks before it collapsed. A couple dozen people were severely injured as a result. What is the quality of those goods?

And finally, just let me ask, if you could—Mr. Chang, in your book, "The Coming Collapse of China," and elsewhere, you have questioned the sustainability of China's debt in the long-term in part due to its inefficient lending to state-owned enterprises.

And I am wondering how the level of indebtedness of African nations, in particular those rated by the Center for Global Development as being potential high risks of distress—namely, Djibouti, Ethiopia, Kenya, others—factor into China's own financial health?

What would be the effect on China's lending institutions of a default or a restructuring and how do you think that might rattle markets globally?

Mr. CHANG. You know, Mr. Chairman, we are seeing—and it's not played out in Africa but certainly being played out in Venezuela where there is somewhere between $17 billion to $20 billion of debt, and to borrow your term, we just don't know the full extent of that debt.

But we do know that China is in difficult straits because they don't know how to do this. Part of it is because maybe of a lack of experience, but also because they realize that the more money they put into Venezuela the more difficult it becomes as a bigger problem and, indeed, in the last year or so, they have not been extending additional advances.

Now, they are going to play this all out in connection with Djibouti, as you mentioned, and also with Tanzania right now with the debt restructuring.

You know, Beijing has a lot of money, but it also has a lot of commitments and this is the whole concept of imperial overstretch, and we see this playing out in China's relations with countries around the world, especially in Africa, where they have gone out and made very large commitments, but have not oftentimes been able to fulfill them, and that is largely because they've got too big ambitions.

They say that they have $3.2 trillion of foreign exchange reserves but that money is not unencumbered. They've been using a fair amount of this money for belt-and-road projects, which are not sustainable.

I practiced law in Hong Kong at a time where anything that could be financed was financed by the private sector. What China is doing with belt-and-road right is financing those things that nobody would have ever touched, and they wouldn't have touched them for a good reason.

So Beijing is going to see all of these projects—not all of them but many of these projects having to be refinanced on terms that are unfavorable to the Chinese largely because these projects are just not economic.

We see this especially in Latin America right now where you've had two very large Chinese projects crater—the Interoceanic Canal at Nicaragua and also the Atlantic to Pacific railroad.

China hasn't done, I think, anything as large as that in Africa, which have been such spectacular failures. But we have seen smaller projects not go forward in similar fashion.

Mr. SMITH. Mr. Castro.

Mr. CASTRO. Thank you all for your testimony today.

Let me ask you all, how much does China use—aside from their projects, right, like the ones they are doing in Latin America and some of the projects in Africa—what kind of development aid do they offer to the countries in the way that United States has USAID, for example?

Mr. MORRIS. I think the common view is that they don't have an aid model. I don't think that's entirely correct. They do have what we'd consider foreign aid. Official development assistance is the terminology.

It is very small relative to the other types of financing they do. It is growing.

Mr. CASTRO. And why do you think that they haven't used that—they haven't adopted the same model? Is it that they can't afford it or they just don't believe in it? What's your best assessment?

Mr. MORRIS. What I would hear from Chinese counterparts over the years consistently is, "We are not a rich country—we are not an aid provider—we ourselves are a poor country."

Now, they've had to evolve that message, as we——

Mr. CASTRO. It's the second largest economy in the world.

Mr. MORRIS. Yes, and both—so the message has evolved but also the reality is changing. They are increasing their levels of foreign aid.

On something like the belt-and-road initiative, which is infrastructure oriented, you are seeing an aid component allocated to things like technical assistance, project preparation.

Mr. CASTRO. Let me ask you—I have a question.

There have been stories recently about cobalt mining in Africa. To what extent do Chinese companies comply with international standards on child labor when extracting natural resources in African countries, such as cobalt mining in the Democratic Republic of Congo? If anybody can address that.

Mr. MESERVEY. You know, the cobalt issue in Eastern DRC is a fascinating one. The Chinese have moved strategically, I would say, to dominate the global supply chain for cobalt.

Cobalt, of course, is a critical mineral in the creation of lithium ion batteries, which may well be extraordinarily important even more so than now if—particularly if driverless cars becomes as big of an industry as many people think it will.

So as far as child labor standards specifically, I am not sure what the Chinese companies that are involved in cobalt mining have for those sorts of standards.

As we have mentioned throughout this hearing, though, there is no doubt that Chinese companies do not subscribe to the same level of labor standards as Western firms do, for instance.

So whether that translates specifically into using child labor at a cobalt mine, I don't know. I wouldn't be surprised if the answer is yes.

Mr. CASTRO. Also, China recently opened its first overseas military base in Djibouti. What do you expect the purpose of this base is and where do you see China's expanding footprint in the region and do you see them expanding militarily in Africa beyond this one base?

Mr. CHANG. Beijing has indicated that it clearly wants to dominate the Indian Ocean and in order to do that it does need logistical bases. And so it's no surprise that their first overseas base is essentially to support the People's Liberation Army Navy and it's no surprise that it's in the Indian Ocean.

The thing that I am concerned about is the Chinese have been thinking about establishing a base at Walvis Bay in Namibia in the southern Atlantic, and what's even more concerning—and I mentioned this before—is Chinese officials have been looking at the Azores.

The United States Air Force has a base. It's called Base Number 4, Lajes, and because of budget cutbacks has been reducing the presence there down to what they call a ghost base.

Then-Chinese Premier Wen Jiabao—I think it was in 2009 when he was going from Santiago, Chile back to Beijing actually didn't fly over the Pacific, as you'd expect. He flew to Lajes and spent a couple days on the island looking at not only the air base but also looking at the port facilities, and there have been, clearly, a lot of discussions between the Chinese and the Portuguese.

So this is a concern because from Lajes, which was a base that would control the mouth of the Atlantic—sorry, the Mediterranean—and also it is closer to Washington, DC, then Pearl Harbor is to Los Angeles.

So it is important for us to make sure that—it's sometimes difficult to tell the Air Force what to do. But it would seem that reducing our commitment to the Azores at a time when the Chinese want to use the Azores doesn't seem to be wise policy in the long term because, clearly, we do not want Chinese planes flying over the Atlantic and threatening the American homeland.

Mr. CASTRO. Thank you.

I yield back.

Mr. SMITH. Mr. Garrett.

Mr. GARRETT. Thank you. I want to touch on something that my colleague, Mr. Castro, spoke to—and I want—and, by the way, I am a listener to the John Batchelor program so it's an honor to get to see you in person—and that is Chinese aid versus U.S. aid and the aid model.

And I want you to tell me if I am wrong and I'll open this up to anybody, but I do have a finite amount of time. And that is that the Chinese have learned very quickly that it's easier to give a lot of money to a few people than it is to give even more to a large number of people.

In other words, I was in an African nation that shall remain nameless for a particular reason wherein the Presidential palace was a wholly financed function of the Chinese Government.

It, obviously, endeared itself ultimately to three families. It was probably about the size of the Rayburn House Office Building and by giving that aid they didn't need to give aid to the people in that country who were living on less than $1 a day.

Is that about right? The Chinese aid model is to pay off the oligarchs because they don't need to worry about the masses if they do that.

Mr. CHANG. Some people have called it big project diplomacy. Build, for instance, as Dr. Plummer has talked about, the headquarters for the African Union. You build a soccer stadium. These are high-profile projects.

The United States does something a little bit different. You know, we have a Peace Corps volunteer here, I guess. You know, the aid is more on a person-to-person level—you know, vaccines, which are important, clean water—these types of things which matter day to day—much more important than the headquarters for a multilateral organization in Addis Ababa.

So I think that we are doing the right thing. It's just a question of whether we should be doing more, and let me just close out by saying that I am privileged to know John Batchelor. So thank you very much.

Mr. GARRETT. Well, I've—as a new resident of the district, I have evolved into a great appreciation for the depth and subject matter expertise that's present in that venue, and I know I've digressed beyond the role of the committee today. But I do think I get analysis there I don't get other places.

As it relates to sort of the neocolonialist tag, which I candidly think is incredibly appropriate—it's been my observation in a very limited period of time and only a couple of different countries in the African continent that the reality is that China is on the ground in a depth that we as Americans and even as members of this body fail to understand as it relates to control of the apparatus that make things go—the infrastructure, if you will.

The cliche that I've heard is that ultimately the infrastructure provided by the Chinese serves the Chinese at the expense of the local population, which looks an awful lot like colonialism to me.

I would invite you to speak to the cliche that the roads that they build run from the resource to the port and whether or not that's the reality or if these—if these projects and "investments" actually serve the local populaces, and I would speak to that for perspective, for example, to the story that was in Bloomberg 6 days ago with regard to the Chinese garment manufacturing endeavors in Ethiopia and then the treatment of the workers therein without even digressing into child labor circumstances in China, which they've told us have changed but we have anecdotal and real evidence that indicate they haven't.

So the infrastructure investment that the Chinese tout in the developing world is that to serve the developing world or is that to serve the Chinese, based on—and again, anybody chime in.

Again, Mr. Chang, I hold you in extraordinarily high regard. I have three other awesome people here, including Dr. Plummer, who's got a Woodson fellowship at UVA, which is in my district. So you're awesome.

So anybody—the Chinese investment in infrastructure—is it serving these developing nations or is it serving China?

Ms. PLUMMER. Well, I think it all depends on the project. So your first question when you asked the scope of the infrastructure, who does it serve, you mentioned a project—the Presidential palace.

You find that the Chinese Government tends to be very responsive to what African elites request. So if there is an election year and an elite—a representative says, hey, I need a road built between these two towns—it's an election year—will you be able to deliver that project, of course, it's not free. There is a loan taken out. Leaders in China have been praised for being responsive in that way.

So it's up to the African leadership to make certain requests. So——

Mr. GARRETT. Let me interrupt, not by disrespect and not to even disagree.

The autocratic regime is a lot more responsive, right, than a laboriously democratic——

Ms. PLUMMER. Absolutely. Absolutely.

Mr. GARRETT. But go ahead.

Ms. PLUMMER. So to answer your question, do the—does the local population benefit from the infrastructure—it all depends on the quality of leadership and whether the leadership within that country works autonomously from their population or if they work to benefit their population. So it all depends.

In terms of the large-scale transport infrastructure models and, to some extent, the power infrastructure models, geographers have gone in and mapped out where the roads, the railways, where the ports are being situated.

And yes, you find that it's a two-way street. They benefit the extractive sectors but also they are intended to get Chinese-made products into hard-to-get places within the African interior.

So it serves that dual purpose. But you also find that some of the aid is within the agricultural sector so to teach farmers how to build rice paddies. You have medical doctors that have been dispatched. You have teachers that have been dispatched to different areas. So it's a lot broader than just the large-scale infrastructure.

Mr. GARRETT. I would say this. I mean, the race is a manifest to sort of—there is almost a Sino supremacist sort of attitude amongst a segment of the Chinese leadership—that they are just better than everybody else and that they are doing everybody a favor by virtue of gracing them with their presence, which I think hearkens back to what we saw coming out of Europe for a couple centuries.

But that's troubling in a world where I think we should get back to the King model of content of character versus color of skin, and when it manifests itself in foreign policy—and I think China is not the only instance where this happens, but we aren't talking about some other regions right now that some of you all might have some expertise in—that becomes worse.

Let me ask you a rhetorical based on essentially my opinion, and let me give it to Joshua and Scott, and then conclude, because you all have been very indulgent.

The U.S. model of international aid is the superior model if it is in a world where the individuals in receipt of the aid have self-determination.

In other words, we give aid to the end user—the person who might lack a meal. I am a huge champion of McGovern-Dole, of educating women, to reduce radicalism, and create economic opportunity. Not because I like women better than men but because we see patterns where educated women create greater opportunity, reduce radicalism, and lift the society, right—that if you take 50 percent of your population and disenfranchise them then, ultimately, you never get to be as good as you can be.

So when the end user is self-determinative and our aid goes to the end user then our model works. But where there are autocratic regimes, where there are dictatorial regimes, the Chinese model works because essentially—and you can call them priority projects or whatever you want to call them—but it's buying off the people at the top so as to extract benefit from essentially the sweat of the people at the bottom.

Is that an accurate, in your opinion, Joshua and—or Mr. Meservey—I am dodging your last name because I don't want to mispronounce it—and Mr. Morris?

Mr. MESERVEY. Yes, I think there is a lot of truth to that. In my written testimony, I called corruption a Chinese competitive advantage on the continent.

We have the Foreign Corrupt Practices Act, as we have already talked about during this hearing, and you will go to prison if you're American and you do the sorts of things that Chinese firms are frequently willing to do on the continent.

And it's not just the Chinese, of course, but they are—they are prime perpetrators. And I think the more fundamental issue is that governance is hugely important, as your question referenced, and fundamentally the blame for striking a lot of irresponsible deals lies with governments in Africa and they are to blame for signing these terrible contracts—for allowing themselves to be bought off in some situations.

So I think our U.S. engagement, the aid model, should focus on improving governance on the continent because also even poverty has very strong links to governance. The MCC is a really positive model because it rewards good governance.

So I think that's the direction in which U.S. policy should be going on these issues.

Mr. GARRETT. Mr. Morris.

Mr. MORRIS. So, Congressman, I would certainly agree with you completely on sort of core principles and values that are embodied in what we do internationally that look very different from China.

That said, I would say that if you look at programs like PEPFAR, you know, tremendous strides we have made through that program in incidence of disease and, frankly, irrespective of—I mean, in a lot of different kinds of countries and I think it was really important not to be too restrictive about where we choose to try to make progress in an area like that.

And then on the question of infrastructure, I think it is just—you know, it is a fundamental driver of growth in economies today and, again, that's irrespective of political models.

I think you're right, though, that at the end of the day, the political models bear directly on how that goes when you do actually engage.

But I do think, you know, with our model of leading on global health issues, on humanitarian issues, disaster response, it's critical that we are there when there is a need and find ways to work even when governance is challenging.

Mr. GARRETT. It's amazing, and I say this as an aside—and I thank the chair for his indulgence—but to ask the opinion of George W. Bush in Africa versus in America, right, because we did stuff that helped human beings and they—and they get it.

So without advocating on behalf of a particular administration, when you help people you help America, and when you empower people and create hope, then we reduce radicalization and, as McMaster said, we buy fewer bombs.

Having said that, I served in the military. I want to have a strong military. I don't want to have to use it. We should never aspire to use it.

Thank you, guys, immensely.

Mr. SMITH. Thank you, Mr. Garrett.

Just to conclude, I do have one final question. You know, in my own home state of New Jersey, our former U.S. attorney, Christopher Christie, was able, when he looked at corruption within our own state, to put about 130 politicians, both Democrats and Republicans, behind bars over an 8-year period as he served as U.S. attorney.

Remember, there was a book written, called "The Soprano State," that really showed that corruption is in so many places.

So when we talk about it overseas, we need to look in the mirror. It's here as well. You, Mr. Chang, talked about some of the dealings between Beijing and African states being tainted by corruption.

I co-chair the Helsinki Commission. In 2000 there was a big conference—we have one every year. It's an annual conference—in Bucharest.

The theme of it was that corruption is the hijacker of democracies, and it seems to me that when there is no Foreign Corrupt Practices Act to hold the bad players to account and bags of money are showing up, it has a coercive and, I think, a totally debilitating impact on democracy, which we want every African country—every country in the world—to enjoy the benefits of a robust democracy.

If any of you would like, as we conclude, to speak to that issue. And I remember in Bucharest, we were talking a lot of the emerging democracies and some of whom are going the wrong way, sadly—Russia being probably chief among them—and, of course, the kleptocracy there and the oligarchs have stolen so much, robbed the people of so much there, and Putin is walking point on that.

So if you could speak to that issue, because I think on the intermediate, long-term, short-term as well, you know, we want Africa to thrive. You can't thrive when you have corruption.

Mr. CHANG. Mr. Chairman, I thought—what I thought was really striking was that in the era of Hu Jintao, the predecessor to Xi Jinping, his son was implicated in a bribery scandal in Tanzania for the sale of airports scanners, I believe that it was, and this indicates that this is not just some Chinese businessman being caught—China bribed an African official.

This goes to the—this went to the top of the Chinese political system, and I think people understood that this was the nature of China in Africa, in other places as well.

And so you see this replicated. You know, as Dr. Plummer said, you got to look at it country by country. But nonetheless, this was one very glaring example of the son of a Chinese political leader bribing officials in Africa and being withdrawn out of Africa to avoid embarrassment in Beijing.

Mr. SMITH. Dr. Plummer.

Ms. PLUMMER. Chairman Smith, thank you so much for bringing up the corruption issue.

I just want to reiterate the illicit financial flows. Billions of dollars are leaving Africa every year and they are being held in banks in Europe, in the United States, and in the Caribbean, and the United States can play a role in helping to recover that money and repatriate it back to the continent.

So I think that's something that's very tangible that we can play a role because we have robust institutions to be able to investigate where this money is going and where it's being held.

Mr. SMITH. Mr. Morris, what role should we play?

Mr. MORRIS. I just want to agree with Dr. Plummer. I think this is—I mean, it's not what we consider by any means traditional foreign aid but it's a—it's a critical function of the U.S. Government that, you know, we are providing a good to the global community in this regard by acting aggressively in this area.

Mr. MESERVEY. I'll give a quick example to supplement what Dr. Plummer said.

The Vice President of Equatorial Guinea is the son of the President there actually, and he has had luxury vehicles and mansions seized all over the world now because—in Europe and in the U.S.—because those governments decided to go after him.

There is a plethora of opportunities to do that sort of thing. The U.S. has particular leverage with dual citizens who populate governments in Somalia and South Sudan. So that's an obvious—another area.

And it's not just China that engages in this activity. Gulf States are very bad in this way as well.

Mr. SMITH. Thank you so very much for sharing your insights and wisdom with the subcommittee.

The hearing is adjourned.

[Whereupon, at 3:52 p.m., the committee was adjourned.]

APPENDIX

MATERIAL SUBMITTED FOR THE RECORD

SUBCOMMITTEE HEARING NOTICE
COMMITTEE ON FOREIGN AFFAIRS
U.S. HOUSE OF REPRESENTATIVES
WASHINGTON, DC 20515-6128

Subcommittee on Africa, Global Health, Global Human Rights, and International Organizations
Christopher H. Smith (R-NJ), Chairman

March 6, 2018

TO: MEMBERS OF THE COMMITTEE ON FOREIGN AFFAIRS

You are respectfully requested to attend an OPEN hearing of the Committee on Foreign Affairs to be held by the Subcommittee on Africa, Global Health, Global Human Rights, and International Organizations in Room 2172 of the Rayburn House Office Building (and available live on the Committee website at http://www.ForeignAffairs.house.gov):

DATE: Wednesday, March 7, 2018

TIME: 2:00 p.m.

SUBJECT: China in Africa: The New Colonialism?

WITNESSES: Mr. Gordon Chang
Author

Mr. Joshua Meservey
Senior Policy Analyst
Africa and the Middle East
The Heritage Foundation

Mr. Scott Morris
Senior Fellow
Center for Global Development

Anita Plummer, Ph.D.
Assistant Professor
Department of African Studies
Howard University

By Direction of the Chairman

COMMITTEE ON FOREIGN AFFAIRS

MINUTES OF SUBCOMMITTEE ON _Africa, Global Health, Global Human Rights, and International Organizations_ HEARING

Day___*Wednesday*___Date____*March 7, 2018*___Room________*2172*________

Starting Time ___*2:03pm*___ Ending Time ___*3:54pm*___

Recesses |____| (___to___) (___to___) (___to___) (___to___) (___to___) (___to___)

Presiding Member(s)
Chairman Smith

Check all of the following that apply:

Open Session ☑
Executive (closed) Session ☐
Televised ☐

Electronically Recorded (taped) ☐
Stenographic Record ☑

TITLE OF HEARING:
China in Africa: The New Colonialism?

SUBCOMMITTEE MEMBERS PRESENT:
Ranking Member Bass, Rep. Bera, Rep. Garrett, Rep. Castro

NON-SUBCOMMITTEE MEMBERS PRESENT: *(Mark with an * if they are not members of full committee.)*

Rep. Francis Rooney, Rep. Chabot

HEARING WITNESSES: Same as meeting notice attached? Yes ☑ No ☐
(If "no", please list below and include title, agency, department, or organization.)

STATEMENTS FOR THE RECORD: *(List any statements submitted for the record.)*

-Smith: Written statement prepared by Samantha Custer, AidData at the College of William & Mary

-Smith: "China-Kenya Relationship: Influence of Money & Growth of Corruption" by Rev. Abel Oriri, LPCC-S, NCC, Pastor Heights Fellowship Church, Cleveland, Ohio

-Smith: Written Statement by Daniel Asaah, Ghanaian Politician/Entrepreneur

TIME SCHEDULED TO RECONVENE __________
or
TIME ADJOURNED __________

Subcommittee Staff Associate

Material submitted for the record by the Honorable Christopher H. Smith, a Representative in Congress from the State of New Jersey, and chairman, Subcommittee on Africa, Global Health, Global Human Rights, and International Organizations

Written statement prepared by Samantha Custer, AidData at the College of William & Mary

To: Chairman and Members of the House Foreign Affairs Committee, Subcommittee on Africa, Global Health, Global Human Rights, and International Organizations
From: Samantha Custer, Director of Policy Analysis, AidData, College of William & Mary
Date: March 5, 2018
Re: Written Statement for the Hearing on "China in Africa: the New Colonialism?"

Foreign aid accounts for less than one percent of the US national budget, but the benefits it generates on behalf of the American people are notoriously difficult to measure. In the absence of clear evidence, it is easy to discount uncertain future gains in enhanced global security and bargaining power with other countries. US taxpayers will get a greater return reforming, not slashing, their investments in foreign aid.

Historically the largest bilateral provider of official development assistance, a reduced foreign aid budget will likely dilute US global influence and undercut efforts to promote peace, prosperity, and liberal democracy abroad. If the US follows through on its rhetoric and scales back its global footprint, China may be well positioned to step into the breach and cement its role as a preferred donor and lender to the developing world.

Nowhere is this jockeying for influence more evident than in Africa. There is much conjecture about how China uses its overseas investments to influence the domestic and foreign policy choices of countries throughout the region. The "rogue donor" narrative is pervasive in speculating that China gives to corrupt regimes, extracts natural resources, exploits human rights, and is in direct competition with the US.

Yet, it is unclear how much of this speculation is myth versus fact. Fortunately, we now have much better data available to substantiate China's *actual* global development footprint and its influence with African leaders using two novel data sources collected by AidData – a research lab at the College of William & Mary in Virginia.

In this statement, I highlight what China is spending, why, and to what effect in Africa. I also discuss several implications for how the US should deploy its foreign policy tools, including the development assistance budget, to maximize its influence in delivering policy change abroad and ensuring accountability for results with taxpayers at home.

MONEY: HOW DO WE QUANTIFY CHINA'S GLOBAL DEVELOPMENT SPREE?

China is quite opaque regarding how it deploys official overseas investments. It does not typically disclose which countries benefit from its assistance, nor provide any granular project level details on the nature of those investments. To close this evidence gap, AidData assembled the most comprehensive and detailed source of publicly available project level information on China's global development footprint to date (via aiddata.org/china). Triangulating information from multiple data sources — media reports, academic papers, government ministry and embassy websites, case studies

Written statement prepared by Samantha Custer, AidData at the College of William & Mary

and field research – our database captures **US$354 billion in Chinese global official finance investments between 2000-2014, including detailed information on 4300 discrete projects.**

Many Western countries ascribe to the Organization for Economic Cooperation and Development's view of aid as limited to official development assistance — which must be primarily intended for development and highly concessional in its terms, including a grant element of more than 25 percent. However, emerging donors such as China, Brazil, and India argue that this Western notion of "aid" does not fit their approach and discounts other official finance contributions that are less concessional or serve a mixed purpose of advancing development along with commercial or diplomatic ends.

These distinctions matter: **the US dwarfs China in official development assistance, but the two countries have roughly similarly sized overall official finance portfolios overall.** If we looked at aid alone, we would not be able to accurately gauge the full extent of China's global development footprint. For this reason, AidData collects information on both types of Chinese overseas investments: (1) official development assistance (ODA or "aid"); and (2) other official flows (OOF).

Globally, **China has been steadily increasing its overall official financing invested in other countries, exceeding the US since 2009.** Nonetheless, Chinese official finance is less concessional than that of other large players like the US, since the vast majority of China's assistance does not meet the level of concessionality to be considered ODA. See Figures 1 and 2 for more information.

Seven of the top 10 recipients of Chinese "aid" (ODA) were in Africa, but its other official flows (OOF) are more geographically dispersed. Cote d'Ivoire, Ethiopia, Zimbabwe, Cameroon, Nigeria, Tanzania, and Ghana collectively received US$23.3 billion in official development assistance from China between 2000 and 2014. Africa is less of a priority for China when it comes to its more commercial or diplomatically focused other official financing. Angola is the lone African country in the top ten recipients of Chinese OOF, receiving $13.4 billion.

Consistent with its signature effort to set up the Asia Infrastructure Investment Bank, China's official financing reveals that it is making big bets in the infrastructure sector. **The lion's share of China's investments globally between 2000 and 2014 were in energy (US$134.1 billion), transportation and storage (US$88.8 billion), telecommunications projects (US$16.9 billion) and mining, construction and industry (US$ 30.3B).**

Written statement prepared by Samantha Custer, AidData at the College of William & Mary

Figure 1.

What's Included in China's Official Finance?

China's official finance is less concessional than that of other large players

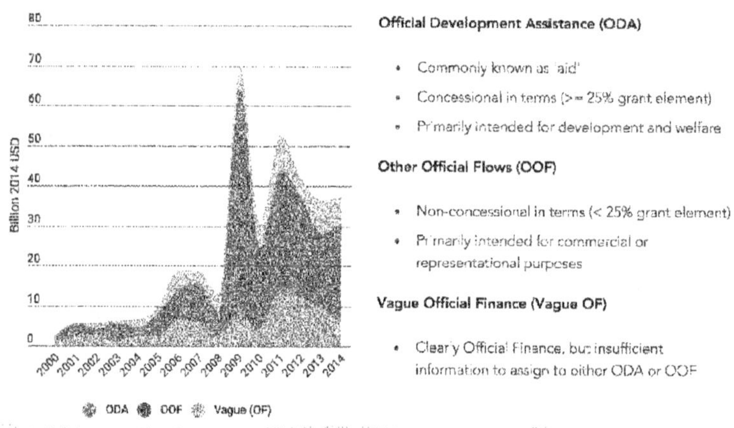

Source: AidData. 2017. Global Chinese Official Finance Dataset, Version 1.0. Retrieved from *http://aiddata.org/china*

Figure 2.

How Does China Compare Against the United States?

Similar sized portfolios with very different compositions

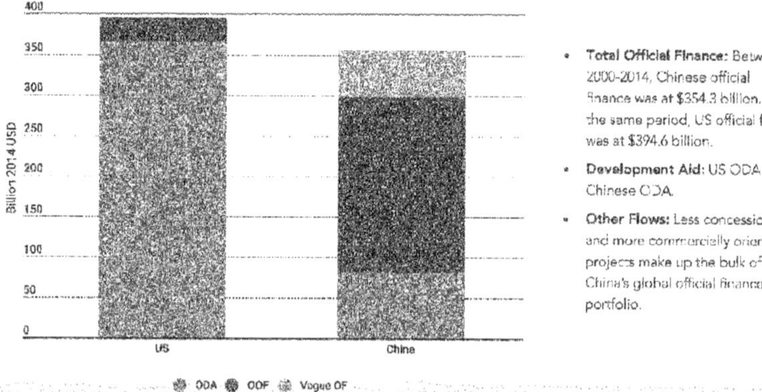

Source: AidData. 2017. Global Chinese Official Finance Dataset, Version 1.0. Retrieved from *http://aiddata.org/china*

Written statement prepared by Samantha Custer, AidData at the College of William & Mary

MOTIVATION: WHAT APPEARS TO BE DRIVING CHINA'S OFFICIAL FINANCE INVESTMENTS?

Turning from the numbers to some of the possible explanations that might be driving their investment patterns, China appears to play by different rules when it comes to deploying these different flows. In an AidData working paper entitled "Apples and Dragon Fruits", a team of researchers empirically tested which factors appear to drive Chinese official finance investments (see Dreher et al, 2015). Below I highlight a few important takeaways from this research to understanding why and how China engages with African leaders through its official finance investments.

In several respects, the evidence busts several popular myths regarding Chinese aid. **Chinese ODA appears to be more responsible and responsive to need than we typically give it credit for in that it is pro-poor, given without strings attached, and is regime agnostic.** Chinese development assistance tends to go towards poorer countries. Contrary to the conventional wisdom, it does not appear that China is giving aid with strings attached in order to access natural resources or commercial ties. Nor is Chinese aid going disproportionately to authoritarian or corrupt regimes (Dreher et al., 2015).

However, **there is an important exception where China's aid giving appears to follow the prevailing narrative of quid pro quo – buying votes.** If African countries voted with China in the UN General Assembly an extra 10% of the time, they would get an 86% bump in official development assistance on average, according to the Dreher et al. (2015) study. In other words, if a country aligned with China's foreign policy positions in the United Nations, that opened up the door to substantially more aid than if they did not.

A second AidData working paper, entitled "Aid, China, and Growth", by Dreher et al. (2017) illuminates another important point. **In its deployment of other official flows, China appears to hue more closely to the self-interest narrative. Chinese OOF primarily goes to countries that have greater capacity to repay loans, have larger natural resource endowments, are more corrupt, and are considered valued trading partners.**

What are the downstream effects of this increasing volume of official financing investments made by China in Africa? The prognosis is mixed – there are important differences between the two types of Chinese assistance, not only in how these flows are targeted, but also their effects and effectiveness, according to the Dreher et al. (2017) study. On a positive note, **Chinese official development assistance, narrowly defined, appears to bolster economic growth in African countries and does not necessarily undermine the effectiveness of Western assistance.** Ironically, **however, the commercial and diplomatic intentions of China's other official flows, does not appear to be translating into greater economic growth on the ground.**

Written statement prepared by Samantha Custer, AidData at the College of William & Mary

LEVERAGE: TO WHAT EXTENT IS CHINA INFLUENCING POLICY IN OTHER COUNTRIES?

So what do policymakers in Africa make of China's growing development footprint in their countries? In addition to following the money, AidData also measures the influence of foreign governments and international organizations in shaping the domestic policy priorities of public, private, and civil society leaders in low- and middle-income countries. To this end, we fielded two surveys of policymakers in 126 countries in 2014 and 2017 to understand whom these leaders listen to – and why? The 2014 survey results are publicly available via aiddata.org/listening-to-leaders and we will be publishing the analysis of the 2017 survey in April 2018.

Nearly 7500 and 3200 leaders responded to AidData's 2014 and 2017 policymaker surveys, respectively. These survey respondents assessed the agenda-setting influence of over 100 bilateral and multilateral donors on a scale of 0 (less influence) to 5 (more influence). Analyzing their responses, we can learn a lot about how China's charm offensive is perceived vis-à-vis the US among African leaders. While the 2017 study is not yet published, I will share some preliminary insights we're gleaning from the data.

Popular arguments that China is rapidly eclipsing US interests and influence worldwide may be overstated. **As of 2017, China still trailed the US in agenda setting influence with leaders in low- and middle-income countries** (Custer et al., forthcoming). **Sixty-five percent of leaders viewed China as quite or very influential in informing their domestic policy priorities compared with over 80 percent for the US in 2017.** However, another interpretation could be that China is a relatively young donor and is just getting started.

In Africa, the picture is a bit more nuanced: **in 2017, the US still had a strong influence edge over China with leaders in sub-Saharan Africa, but is falling behind in the Middle East and North Africa.** The US surpasses China's influence in several policy areas: governance, social, environmental policy among them. Meanwhile, **China was viewed as quite influential among leaders working on economic policy, a policy domain in which it is in a virtual dead heat with the US, and it surpassed US influence in infrastructure for the first time in 2017.**

These survey results tell us that **the substantial investments made by China in the infrastructure sector are indeed paying off — in terms of agenda-setting influence with world leaders.** Finally, in **comparing scores from 2014 and 2017, there is a clear indication that China is rapidly gaining ground when it comes to agenda-setting influence** with policymakers in low- and middle-income countries. More on this is still to come with AidData's forthcoming publication analyzing the full survey results in April 2018.

IMPLICATIONS: HOW SHOULD THE US RESPOND TO CHINA'S GROWING

Written statement prepared by Samantha Custer, AidData at the College of William & Mary

FOOTPRINT AND INFLUENCE IN AFRICA?

1. US development assistance can become more focused and effective, but should not cede its "ground game" in cultivating long-term partnerships and influence with African leaders

Money may not buy love, but it does give donors a seat at the table with policymakers in low- and middle-income countries. On average, donors with deep pockets such as the United States, World Bank, and the EU are seen as more influential in shaping the policy agenda than less well endowed ones (Custer et al., 2015). Similarly, we find that **China appears to hold most sway with leaders from countries that are heavily dependent on its grants and loans, perhaps another reason for the US to think twice about pulling back on its assistance to African countries.**

The strength of a donor's "ground game" – its local presence and direct interactions with host government officials – informs how in-country decision-makers assess its influence. US agencies may find it advantageous to take a cue from small bilateral donors that have identified a bounded number of priority countries with whom to cultivate deeper, long-term relationships. Greater selectivity would enable overstretched and under-resourced agencies like USAID to focus on fewer countries and provide them with targeted policy advice and assistance.

However, closing USAID missions to achieve an arbitrary budget reduction target is not prioritization, nor does it necessarily indicate a ramping up of efforts in countries where the US has a comparative advantage. Instead, **Congressional and executive-branch leaders should give US agencies the mandate to rebalance their portfolio** based upon a clear-eyed assessment of three criteria: (i) the potency of its agenda-setting influence in a given country; (ii) objective measures of need and opportunity for US assistance to make a positive difference; and (iii) strategic relationships and alliances that the US must consider when it comes to deploying aid as a foreign policy tool.

2. Foreign policy tools work better together than apart: the US should continue to invest in public diplomacy efforts alongside overseas development investments to amplify its influence

Beyond overseas development investments, there is a clear indication that public diplomacy tools can work together with development assistance to amplify influence with leaders in African countries. **China had substantially more sway in countries where leaders have had greater interaction with the Chinese Communist party** (tested using the number of times a delegation of leaders from a given country visited the CCP between 1998-2014). Notably, **China had less influence with countries that had a greater number of leaders who were educated in the US and Fulbright scholars** studying in the US (between 1949 and 2004). In addition to the cultural and educational exchange programs that target elites, there is also still a place for

Written statement prepared by Samantha Custer, AidData at the College of William & Mary

informational diplomacy and outreach with the general public. We find that **China had the most sway in countries where the general public views its development model favorably** (tested using Afrobarometer data).

Congressional and executive-branch leaders should resist the urge to subordinate development assistance to diplomacy and defense programs or vice versa. The US should strengthen its capacity in all of these areas if it is to maintain and amplify its influence in African countries. Instead of pitting US diplomacy and development programs against each other in a competition for scarce resources and policymaker attention, **Congressional leaders should encourage the leadership of USAID, MCC, State, and other relevant agencies to cultivate mutually reinforcing linkages between all of the foreign policy tools at their disposal.** There is good reason to believe that such a whole-of-government approach may be more effective than disjointed efforts to maintain and amplify US influence in African countries.

ABOUT AIDDATA

AidData, a research lab at the College of William & Mary, tracks over *40 trillion dollars* in financing for development to understand who is funding, what, where and to what effect. It also fields surveys of over *55,000 policymakers* worldwide to quantify how external money and ideas shape domestic reforms in low- and middle-income countries. Using rigorous methods, cutting-edge tools, and granular data, AidData equips policymakers and practitioners to effectively target, monitor, and evaluate development investments.

"CHINA-KENYA RELATIONSHIP: INFLUENCE OF MONEY & GROWTH OF CORRUPTION"

By

Rev. Abel Oriri, LPCC-S, NCC

Pastor Heights Fellowship Church

Cleveland, Ohio

Paper presented to

THE UNITED STATES HOUSE OF CONGRESS SUB COMMITTEE ON AFRICA

WASHINGTON, DC

March 6, 2018

"CHINA-KENYA RELATIONSHIP: INFLUENCE OF MONEY & GROWTH OF CORRUPTION"

The Definition of Corruption:

According to Webster dictionary, corruption is defined as follows: "dishonest or illegal behavior especially by powerful people (such as government officials or police officers); inducement to wrong by improper or unlawful means (such as bribery) – the corruption of government officials; departure from the original or from what is pure or correct – the corruption of a text the corruption of computer files." When it comes to dealing with China, the Kenyan government has always been making shady arrangements at the very top, often in the president's or deputy president's offices. Contracts are believed to be greased with monetary bribes and other enticements like expense-paid shopping trips to China and scholarships there for the children of the elite. Adding to the opacity, China typically favors its state-owned companies for African projects and bypasses open, competitive bidding procedures.

According to the New York Times, the Chinese money and the growth of corruption have peppered the continent with newly built stadiums, airports, hospitals, highways, and dams. But as Africans are beginning to fully recognize, these projects have also left many countries saddled with heavy debts and other problems, from environmental conflict to labor strife. Additionally, Bright and Hruby (2015) noted there is a perception that within Africa, the Chinese are known move quickly with a project once the MOU is signed involving a contract and can be "on the ground in a week" to do the feasibility study in days. The truth is that the study itself is not comprehensive, but merely analyzes the cost of the project. That is the reason African governments say that American firms take so long to do a feasibility study, and the Chinese will do it in two months.

Dr. David Ndii, an Oxford scholar economist, Rhodes scholar and Eisenhower fellow, who is considered one of world's most influential economist, has written extensively about governance and warned Kenya repeatedly on the dangers of graft, greed, and attractive Chinese money and its corrupting influence. This money poses a great danger to the recipient country's economic gains. The loans are more expensive for countries such as Kenya to repay because of the terms, corruption, and lack of clear planning. The only winner is Chinese government, workers, and Chinese banks.
The US Secretary, Rex Tillerson made the following remarks as he prepared to leave for Africa, in his speech at George Mason University. He said, "Chinese investment has the potential to address Africa's infrastructure gap, but its approach has led to mounting debt and few if any jobs in most countries." Tillerson went on to suggest that Chinese loans are coupled with political and fiscal pressure, which endanger the Africa's natural resources and the long-term economic and continent's political stability. Dr. Ndii's has been brave enough to expose some of the corrupt, unethical deals between Chinese and the Kenyan governments, especially on the contract involving mega projects such as SGR that may sound a death trap to Kenya's economy to benefit the banks. The Chinese easy money is expensive in the long-run and will cost Kenya's tax payers

billions and billions of US Dollars to repay. Dr. Ndii's has given a detailed account of questionable practices between China and Kenya government officials involving the biggest Chinese financed project in Kenya, the Standard Gauge Railway financed and built by a Chinese contractor. The phase one is completed, the constructed railway line connects Mombasa to Nairobi at Sh327 billion (USD$ 3 billion), same as the Ethiopian line that was built by the same Chinese company almost at the same time, but the Kenya one is more than 100 km shorter. The questions that Kenyans are asking are: Has Ethiopia built an inferior line or is Kenya not receiving value for money or is our money being stolen through corruption? These corrupt business deals are raising some serious economic, social, ethical, and political issues that Chinese and Kenyan government officials must answer. Kenya's love for China is sliding and is openly concerned by the level of corruption brought by Chinese money. It is sad to see that poverty is growing, yet politicians and government officials are competing to own helicopters that have become the mode of transportation for the political class. China plays a big part in corrupting leaders to gain business advantages through corruption within Africa, especially in Kenya.

CHINESE INVESTMENT:

The continued growth of Chinese investment in Africa is generally welcomed by Africans, but countries such as Kenya are concerned and worried about the long-term consequences to the development of Africa. The political tensions are building, amidst plundering of resources by few corrupt Kenyans with Chinese government and businesses with no moral campus to guide their practices. The objective of this investment is making money with no regards to the people's welfare. 1 would like to outline five key areas that Kenyans have identified that are associated with Chinese corrupt practices in Kenya:

1) Chinese Loans: China is known to give loans to corrupt African government without asking any hard questions to these countries and their corrupt leaders. It is a common knowledge that loans are given above the project cost and you can guess where the rest goes. For an example, a project may cost only $ 10,000,000, but China will approve $ 20,000,000 as requested by corrupt governments officials.

2) Loan Repayment: China demands collateral and will insist that their loan money be paid first. We have witnessed where they come to the country to demand payment. In the case of Sri Lanka, when they could not pay back the loan China took over their Sea Port.

3) Highest Interest Rate: Chinese loans are like the US pay day loans. They tick these African countries and burden them with money and interest on the loans they can't pay back. If nothing is done, we can see China taking over countries like Kenya!

4) Questionable Projects: China is moving away from coal, yet financing a coal mining project in Lamu, Kenya. The locals are against the project for environmental, economic, and health reasons, but sadly the corrupt deals shut out any opposing voice!

5) Work Permit: Chinese have become preferred group when it comes to work permit. The ambassador of India made a formal complaint to Kenyan government because their nationals were constantly denied work visa, while Chinese employees were being approved for work permit. The special treatment of Chinese nationals over Indian nationals by Kenyan government was raised by the Indian ambassador to Kenya and wanted to know why Indian nationals were treated differently from Chinese counterpart. Kenyans are also alarmed and protest Chinese influence, especially when such close door deals between Kenya government officials and Chinese nationals within the Nyayo building, where government offices for immigration department are housed. This place is well known for corrupt deals. It is the site

where all visas and work permit and other immigration issues are handled. One leading human right advocate told me and I quote, "40 Chinese nationals can walk into Nyayo house and all of them would be approved for work permit, while other credible nationalities are denied"

CONCLUSION

Because research is scarce on the impact of corruption between China and Africa dealings, the effects of corrupt dealing are common knowledge in Africa and requires more documentation. The African governments use all their powers to silence any protest. We see millionaires and billionaires created overnight with no record of work or business earnings to show the sources of their new wealth. These leaders make numerous trips to China each year for "official business" while at home they display wealth that no one is aware of their sources, and they cannot tell you how they got the wealth. They are not open to democratic practices and no one knows how they report their taxes. These leaders and their business associates will do anything to stay in power with the assistance of their Chinese collaborators who are willing and ready to come to their rescue during election season to finance new projects or relaunch old ones to fool the citizens of their worth for reelection.

Finally, China must do the following:

a) China must level the playing and follow the golden rule in Africa and not see Africa as a place to extract raw materials and leave the people in debt that our children cannot pay.

b) China must abide by the constitution of Kenya and follow business ethics in their engagement with nationals.

c) China must avoid secret deals that regular Kenyans do not understand and avoid loans that the children of Kenya will not even be able to pay back.

d) China must stop inflating projects to bribe corrupt government officials to award them contracts.

e) China cannot turn a blind eye to human right abuses and democratic principles and must not keep sustain despots and crooks in power to exploit Africa.

REFERENCE

Bright, J., & Hruby, A. (2015). *The next Africa: An emerging continent becomes a global powerhouse*. Macmillan.

http:wledge.wharton.upenn.edu/article/chinas-investments-in-africa-whats-the-real-story/

http://www.tbo.com/ap/national/tillerson-says-china-encourages-dependency-in-africa-ap_national1961e4039b5244fcbe39189f82d5adf2

https://www.jamiiforums.com/threads/kenya-vs-ethiopia-sgr-compared-thanks-to-the-fellow-who-did-this.1133381/

https://www.nytimes.com/2014/05/17/opinion/into-africa-chinas-wild-rush.htmlhttps://www.sde.co.ke/thenairobian/article/2001262494/the-ties-that-bind-dr-david-ndii-to-raila-and-uhuru

MATERIAL SUBMITTED FOR THE RECORD BY THE HONORABLE CHRISTOPHER H. SMITH, A REPRESENTATIVE IN CONGRESS FROM THE STATE OF NEW JERSEY, AND CHAIRMAN, SUBCOMMITTEE ON AFRICA, GLOBAL HEALTH, GLOBAL HUMAN RIGHTS, AND INTERNATIONAL ORGANIZATIONS

oasuah137@gmail.com
P.O. Box LG 1002 Legon
+233 24 473 9386
+233 20 141 4980

Written Statement on the Subject; China in Africa: The New Colonialism? To Members of the Committee on Foreign Affairs.

By: Daniel Asaah
Ghanaian Politician/Entrepreneur

"The Chinese are coming" is a popular mantra when describing Chinese investments in Africa. Over the years, China's economic growth has positioned them atop when it comes to aiding growth in Africa especially, Ghana. In less than eight years, China-Africa trade increased from $10 billion to over $100 billion. After 2012, two-way trade between Africa and China exceeded $120 billion and is still growing significantly. As we speak today, Africa is now the fourth largest destination of Chinese Investment.

For a country like Ghana, since gaining independence from Britain in 1957, Ghana has been very proactive in originating and implementing development programmes, for which it has received substantial donor support, especially since the 1980s. The country has also remained relatively stable in the West African Sub-region troubled by conflicts, compared to neighbors like Nigeria, Cote d'Ivoire, Ghana is a resource-abundant country, endowed with gold, timber and cocoa (which are its leading exports), and enjoys a favorable coastal position and political stability.

African countries, with specific reference to Ghana has since received immense support from the Chinese of which this piece seems to highlight. Most often these supports have been to the advantage of Ghana but have been met with some setbacks, all which we will explore.

Ghana and the People's Republic of China (PRC) established official diplomatic ties in 1960. Since then, relations between the two countries have deepened by strong personal relationships between the political elites of the two countries, especially during the era of Nkrumah and Premier Zhou Enlai, and by high-level official visits, including visits by Ghana's President John Kufuor to China in 2002 and China's President Hu to Ghana in 2003, with the latest visit by Vice President, Alhaji Dr. Mahamadu Bawumia upon the invitation of the Chinese government last year.

Ghana, over the years has identified Foreign Direct Investment as a key way to advance its economic growth, this has led to Ghana establishing a lot of bilateral relationship with other countries of which China is no exception.

Over the past 50 years, Ghana has received assistance from China in diverse ways ranging from employment, education to direct investments. To throw more lights on some supports:
Just some months ago, the Vice President of Ghana Dr. Mahamadu Bawumia outlined about 20 solid projects from the Chinese Government to Ghana to the tune of $15billion. In the area of development, China has been of immense help to Ghana;

In a quest to achieve the Sustainable Development Goals by 2030, President Akufo Addo at a meeting with President of the 71st Session of the UN General Assembly, Peter Thompson reiterated government's commitment towards industrial transformation, diversifying agriculture for increased productivity and creating a strong social services sector in the country.

To this end, the President stated that his government had introduced a raft of policy measures aimed at creating an enabling environment for the private sector to flourish. These measures, he added, would shift the focus of Ghana's economy from taxation to production, and, hopefully, make Ghanaian businesses very competitive in West Africa, Africa and beyond.

 On agriculture, the occupational mainstay of the majority of Ghanaians, President Akufo-Addo indicated that initiatives such as the programme for Planting for Food and Jobs, and the one-Village-one-Dam project in the three regions of the North, are the answers to the twin-problem of the migration of youth to city centres. He pointed to the fact that the countries that had done well, even without natural resources, are the countries that had invested in education and skills training.

Education and skills training, he noted, were the most important source of empowering and providing opportunities to the youth to help drive Ghana's development, and in the process create jobs.

China over the years have written off some debts owed her by Ghana. Although debt relief has helped Ghana to make savings on interest payments, the savings made are still small in relation to the enormous challenges facing the country.

While debt relief itself does not bring in substantial, new money for development, rich countries have also reneged on their pledge to increase their official development assistance (ODA) to 0.7% of their gross domestic products, although the UN set such a target some time ago in the 1970s and China can still be found in the list of such countries.

Aside from writing down debt owed to it by Ghana since 1985 by $25 million, China has provided much-needed additional loans to assist Ghana to overcome its development challenges. Since the 1960s, China has assisted Ghana's development with technical support;

grants; and interest-free, interest-subsidized and concessionary loans (buyers' and suppliers' credit). China's ODA to Ghana is very significant and an average Ghanaian who knows the ins and outs of governance appreciates that.

Even as back as 1964 and 1970, China extended a total of $43.5 million in assistance, and the largest single Chinese loan advanced to Ghana between the 1960s and the 1990s was a buyer's credit of $18 million. Since 2001, however, China has become a major development partner for Ghana, concentrating its assistance especially on the development of roads, energy and telecommunications infrastructure, and on technical cooperation (including raising agricultural productivity in Ghana and supplying industrial equipment such as machinery for Ghana's ailing textile sector).

In late 2017 a grant of about RMB100 million for infrastructure development was granted Ghana by China. Ghana government intends to use this monies to acquire about 500 vehicles for the police, about RMB 50 million for the Ghana Armed Forces, 4 patrol boats for the Ghana Navy, Fund construction of 90 bridges across the country, Fund construction of Interchange at 'Point 7' in Tamale which would be the first ever interchange in northern Ghana, Four Interchanges (Sofoline, Oforikrom, PTC Takoradi, Danquah Circle), Ten industrial parks in 10 regions, Construction of the Eastern, and Central Rail Lines including its extension to Paga in the north of the country, the Boankra, Buipe Inland Ports and Pagainland terminal, 910 km of road network and to Build a new Accra Psychiatric Hospital.

Energy crisis has been an enemy for the growth of Ghana as the power outage brought about the closure of many companies and inflated the cost of doing business for the very few who thrived irrespective.

The infamous power outages called "Dumsor" saw China again coming to the aid of Ghana with a $562 million loan from the China Export and Import Bank (Exim Bank) for the construction of a $622 million dam at Bui, located strategically between the north and south of the country.

The Chinese loan was a mixed credit financing arrangement, with 42% being a concessionary loan and the rest are a supplier's credit. The concessionary component of the loan is payable over 20 years at 2% interest per annum.

The construction of the dam increased the country's energy supply capacity from the current 2,000 MW to 6,000 MW in 2015.

Communication is a vital part of living and it plays a very important part in the growth of every country, China has since also been helping Ghana meet its objective of improving telecommunication services and integrating ICT into its development in 3 different aspects.

First and foremost, Beijing has provided a concessionary loan of $30 million to support the first phase of Ghana's National Communication Backbone and E-Government Project. The project is expected to link all 10 regional capitals and about 36 towns on the fiber routes to assist the implementation of Ghana's ICT for development policy, which has three faces.

The first is to expand access to ICT facilities and training across the nation through the creation of community information centers, which are also expected to assist in the country's decentralization program by serving as hubs for government departments in the various districts.

The second aspect of the policy is to develop systems to gather, manage and share information among government Ministries, Departments and Agencies to make the public sector more efficient.
The third focus was to leverage the spread of ICT skills to build a knowledge economy to diversify the economy and expand its employment-generating capacity.

In support of these projects, the UN Development Program helped to established and run the Information Technology Business Incubator Centre in the capital, Accra which is to provide financial, advisory and entrepreneurial training and the necessary business infrastructure to young entrepreneurs to start IT-related businesses, while China is assisting with the construction of a fibre optic cable from Accra in the south to Tamale in the north of Ghana. In addition, China is helping to build the infrastructure necessary to facilitate the expansion of ICT to rural areas through its support for rural electrification to improve the transmission and distribution of electricity to rural Ghana.

In trade, Chinese - Ghanaian trade is said to follow a classic North–South model, with Ghana exporting mainly primary commodities such as cocoa beans; manganese; sawn timber; natural rubber and vegetable products; and metal ores, concentrates and scrap, while importing from China a wide range of manufactured goods, including textiles and clothing, travelling bags, shoes, electronics, machinery and automobiles.

China use to be the second largest exporter to Ghana behind Nigeria some years ago (which supplies Ghana mainly with crude oil), edging out the US and UK.

In recent times with the discovery of light sweet crude oil in Ghana has changed the narrative, China is now becoming Ghana's largest trading partner as many young Ghanaians are eager to travel to china to bring in goods to sell. Notwithstanding, Ghanaian traders have on several occasions demonstrated and rabbled against the influx of Chinese imported goods on our Ghanaian market.

In the mining sector which has also being accompanied with some few challenges. It's on record that Small-scale mining contributes to about 30% of Ghana's total gold output and provides livelihoods to large numbers of people especially those in the rural communities where this mining activities take place. The small-scale gold mining industry has been 'reserved for Ghanaians' by law, they often use fundamental means of extraction.

The last decade has seen a large increase in foreign involvement, especially from Chinese miners. This introduced a higher level of mechanization and increased the scale of mining with consequent degradation of land and water bodies. By 2016, the participation of Chinese citizens in informal mining in Ghana had grown and received such adverse media coverage, that the Government of Ghana was forced to act.

According to a report by the Global Financial Integrity, between 2014 and 2017, more than 1,477 illegal foreign miners were arrested by Ghanaian authorities and more than 3,800 submitted to deportation voluntarily. In June and July 2014, a total of 4,592 Chinese illegal immigrants were deported from Ghana.

The Government of Ghana as part of measures to eradicate the menace of galamsey deployed a team of heavy military personnel on an operation dubbed **#OPERATION VANGUARD#** to some galamsey prone areas to fight the menace.

The operation led to the arrest of a famous Chinese business woman who had been alleged to have been engaged in illegal mining and the sad death of one of the Soldiers, Captain who was part of the tax force deployed to end Galamsey.

The media fraternity in Ghana also launched various campaign programs such as **#Media Coalition against Galamsey# and Operation End Galamsey Now** where it reported cases where illegal mining took place. It also educated the public against the dangers associated with the act.

Findings also suggest that there are serious negative impacts intensified by the involvement of Chinese miners in Ghana.

In the sector of education, it's being reported that more than 4,000 Ghanaians have benefited from various short and long-term training programs in China since 2000 till date under the sponsorship of the Chinese government. In 2016, 1,200 Ghanaians benefitted from Chinese programs, while 912 persons also benefitted in 2017.

This was made known to the media by the Economic and Commercial Counsellor of the Chinese Embassy in Accra, Mr Chai Zhijing, in meeting organized by his office in Accra in December 2017.

In addition, there will be the Upgrading of 42 SHSs into model schools, provision of Teaching and Learning Materials, 228 Buses and 198 Pickup trucks for schools Irrigation and water transmission systems in northern Ghana from the $ 15 billion cash from China.

China in the infrastructure sector have aided Ghana, they even committed a whopping $2 billion to support Ghana's one-district, one factory (ODOF) policy.

China Railway International Group Limited has also signed a Memorandum of Understanding to provide $10 billion to support the components of a massive infrastructure development program spanning the mining, industrial and railway fields.

There will also the 25,000 houses project for the security services, 100,000 social housing units, 25 district hospitals, Western Regional Hospital, Reconstruction and Rehabilitation of 8,286 collapsing classrooms among others.

In conclusion, its palpable the interest of China in Africa and Ghana is beyond the exploration of natural resources here but stems deep to helping elevate the living conditions and standards of the Ghanaian and African.

Even resource-poor African countries are benefitting from China's economic cooperation with Africa. By helping to build productive infrastructure and expand access to new technologies, China is helping Ghana combat poverty in ways that humanitarian aid and the distribution-consumption-focused poverty alleviation strategies do not.

A recent World Bank report notes that technology diffusion helps developing countries reduce poverty, but weak basic infrastructure systems impose a major limitation on the domestic dissemination of a range of technologies that can be employed in many developing countries

The Ghanaian government have acknowledged this support and has in the past taken initiatives to remove bottle necks that hinder trade between Ghana and china.

Moving forward, both parties should put in more efforts to reduce casualties and roadblocks to eliminate or mitigate agitations that have been encountered in the past since this bilateral relation between these two countries have been to the advantage of both.

List of References:

https://www.saiia.org.za/research-reports/268-china-africa-policy-report-no-3-2008/file

https://fsi.stanford.edu/sites/default/files/CISAC_Thesis_Thompson.pdf

https://www.theigc.org/project/the-impact-of-chinese-involvement-in-small-scale-gold-mining-in-ghana/

https://www.myjoyonline.com/business/2017/July-4th/bawumia-outlines-20-projects-from-chinas-15bn.php

https://www.ghanaweb.com/GhanaHomePage/NewsArchive/Over-4-000-Ghanaians-benefit-from-training-in-China-606472

https://www.graphic.com.gh/news/general-news/china-gives-ghana-2bn-to-finance-one-district-one-factory-veep.html

http://www.ghana.gov.gh/index.php/media-center/press-release/1958-the-sustainable-development-goals-sdgs